peter james

A Most Interesting…
International, Bestselling,
Crime/Thriller Author

roid snapshot. The policeman asked if I was certain, so I looked carefully. I was sure. I've never forgotten his face. But the police said he couldn't have touched Tommy. The man had been in jail from Saturday night until Monday morning for drunk and disorderly conduct. He was an ex-con; he'd been in prison for armed robbery. Maybe he'd learned about Tantalus there. Maybe he read a lot when he was locked up. Greek mythology didn't seem standard reading fare for convicts, but why not? It's loaded with crime and gore and revenge.

They never found Tommy. For a while, some thought he'd run away. Soon, people were saying they "feared the worst" had happened. Alex and I stayed closer to home the rest of the summer.

After Tommy disappeared, the whole town aged. People thrive on secrets, and you can't keep them from having secrets them. It's the allure of the furtive. The blackberry man had briefly been my secret. I told myself nothing I might have said would have helped Tommy. I saw a stranger in the blackberry bushes. He scared me and my dog. A vague complaint would annoy the police more than alarm them.

How do you keep children safe? Don't speak to strangers. All parents tell their kids that, but I talked to the blackberry man. Did Tommy talk to someone, too?

A week after Tommy vanished, the head of the John Deere factory sent men and machines to plow under those blackberry bushes. Obliterate them. As if that would help. Dad said the factory head had a son Tommy's age.

The long wound scraped in the dirt gave a new, clear view of the river from the road. By spring, some green had returned. Blackberry plants are hard to kill. Burning or plowing doesn't work. Poison does, but if you poison the ground, you harm other life—a bad idea, especially alongside a river. Within a few years, the briars were back, thick and tangled. What had been wild and welcome turned into weeds, something unwanted. Even years later, whenever we passed by that place, Alex growled. I looked but never lingered.

ABOUT THE AUTHOR:

Pat Tompkins is an editor in the San Francisco Bay Area. Her fiction has appeared in Mslexia, Grievous Angel, KYSO Flash, and other publications.

Peter James has had a most colorful life. His mother, Cornelia James, was Glovemaker to Her Majesty the Queen, running the business with his late father who was a chartered accountant. The firm is today run by his sister, Genevieve and her husband, and still supplies the Royal Family: www.corneliajames.com.

In 1994, Penguin published his novel "Host" both in print and on two floppy disks, now in the Science Museum as the world's first electronic novel. He was accused by critics of causing the death of the novel, no less. Having weathered that crisis in style, adding to his catalog; being the keynote speaker at a conference at UCLA on the future of reading, alongside Steve Jobs and the CEO of Time Warner, and later many other speaking engagement, after-dinner speaking, guest talks on cruise ships, and speeches in support of charities, and at literary festivals around the globe.

Peter is also an animal lover, hosting three dogs, a number of hens, alpac-

as, emus, as well as a large number of ducks.

His first job, he boasts on his Website, was as Orson Welles' house cleaner, a period in his life when he needed money while he attended film school.

His news clipping he wrote was published in 1965, starting off his prodigious career that includes many television and film credits.

When he was seventeen, he won a national BBC short story competition and got to read his story on the air.

His first novel, *Dead Letter Drop* was published in 1981, and from that point until 2005, he remained a renaissance man, juggling multiple endeavors, including the aforementioned family business, film and television projects… and, of course, novels.

Peter reports that, "From 1980-1985 I bought the rights to all 93 Biggles books and was very involved in bringing it to the screen in 1985. The film had a Royal Premiere in the presence of Prince Charles and Princess Diana.

In 2001 he co-founded Movision Entertainment Limited where he was CEO until 2005." Among the thirteen films made, "The Merchant of Venice" starring Al Pacino, "Head in th Clouds" with Penelope Cruz, "the Statement" with Michael Caine, "A Different Loyalty," starring Sharon Stone, among others.

Along the way he has garnered over forty-five awards, many for his crime novels, and cemented his presence in the genre with a slew of bestselling crime and thriller novels.

In 2012, his novel "Perfect Murder" was staged and became a hit play.

To date he has written 35 novels,

most bestsellers, 13 of which feature Detective Superintendent Roy Grace, the star of his crime series.

Q: You've been (more than) around the block with a lengthy career in a variety of writing (television, films, novels, stage plays and more.) If you could only pick one form of writing, which would it be and why?

A: I love writing crime and psychological thrillers because I am fascinated by human behavior. When I was a small child I always knew there were three things I wanted to do in life - write books, make films and race cars! I always felt that motor racing was too frivolous too go into as a profession and that I wanted to contribute

something of value to the world. After thirty years of alternating two day jobs - writing and producing, I realized in 2005, shortly after making the film I'm most proud of, Merchant Of Venice with Al Pacino and Jeremy Irons, that actually, I much prefer writing novels. The problem with films is that they are such a collaborative process, it becomes almost like a committee, but up to 20 people who each believe it is their film! And most of those 20 normally have egos the size of aircraft carriers. When I write a novel it is just me. I don't have to change a single word, if I choose not to (although of course I always respect my agent and my editor's criticism).

Q: Your life experiences have been equally broad, from cleaning Orson Welles' house, to race car driving.

Given your preferred writing genre as a crime author, does your lifestyle come from your stories, or does it provide elements for your stories?

A: I think as a writer every single thing you do in life provides opportunities to draw from for both inspiration for stories and for texture. I find one joy is that it is impossible to be bored even standing in a tedious airline security queue as I'm looking around thinking 'Ah there's a possible future character'.

Q: Whats the worst part of being a wildly successful crime author? The part you detest the most?

A: There's nothing that I detest. I feel the luckiest person in the world to make a living doing what I love, and to have wonderful fans. I guess if there is anything that angers me it is when a reader gives me or, any other author a 1 star Amazon review because the book arrived with the packaging damaged or some equally ridiculous complaint that has nothing to do with the content of the book! And a final thing - I guess the scariest thing about being 'successful' - is every time I start a new book I am terrified that is not going to be as good as the previous ones because I am determined to always try to raise the bar with each book.

Q: You failed mathematics "O-level" exams three times, and your grades in school were less than stellar. And from this you have reached a level of success many people dream of, but rarely

achieve. What turned you around from that student, to your current level of proficiency?

A: I am a great believer in Oscar Wilde's maxim that nothing that is worth knowing can be taught! I think a lot of teachers at school told me they didn't ever think I'd amount to much and I think determination and tenacity to prove them wrong was a big driver.

Q: What is your writing process like? Are you rigid in your approach, schedule, manner?

A: Each book I write it takes me approximately seven months to write the first draft, then a further four months of editing processes. I try to ensure that whatever I'm doing I leave myself time to write 1000 words 6 days a week. I find my best writing time is

early evening, but I also write in the mornings, taking a break from writing in the afternoon to catch up with emails, walk the dogs, or do interviews and research.

I plan a book carefully. It is really the first 20% that I plan in detail, along with the ending, which I always know, to give me a "road map" and the three high points - but after that I like events to happen spontaneously, and for the story to start to take on a life of its own - that is when, for me, the real excitement starts. I believe that if, as a writer, you do not surprise

BOOKS 'N PIECES MAGAZINE
Published by Alt Publishing
Publisher: William Gensburger
Email: Info@BooksNPieces.com
August 2018 Issue
Join our mailing list and join our
special group! http://bit.ly/BNPMailingList

The Publisher's
inkdrops

This issue is packed with content. Some 7 interviews, 4 short-stories, several articles including a new column called "Wine While Writing."

We have book reviews, writing tips, Facebook groups you might enjoy, and a large bookshop which will be expanding even more, and also on our Website.

You are reading this from your print issue purchase from Amazon. This is our way to avoid subscriptions; just buy the issues you want.

Books 'N Pieces Magazine, now well into its second year, started as a free publication in order to attract bestselling authors.

We now have a widespread, global audience from countries such as Canada, the United Kingdom, Australia, Germany, France, Hong Kong (SAR), Singapore, Malaysia, Africa, to name the larger ones, in addition to a solid, and growing, United States audience.

We need to have a revenue stream to survive, PAY WRITERS, which we do at our own expense right now, and expand to include more pages and more stories. Will you help us grow?

Enjoy this issue. Tell your friends. Leave comments on our Website so we know how to improve.

As always, thank you for your support.

William

William Gensburger, *Publisher*

Cover sign: Ljubisa Sujica/123RF.com

Among the Briars

Tantalizing once described how I felt about blackberries. The wild bushes, heavy with fruit, were a gift of summer. But I've lost my taste for them. And summer, which once spelled freedom, now just means hot months to endure.

I'd been feeling grown-up because I had a new role: guardian. The winter before my last carefree summer, I found a stray puppy. According to my father, "All kids should have a pet. It teaches responsibility."

He talked of his boyhood beagle. My mother was pragmatic: "What happens when it throws up on my new carpet?"

I promised to walk him daily and feed him and clean up after him. Failure to do so meant the dog would go to the pound. I realize now that my parents wouldn't have carried through with that threat.

When they agreed to let him stay, I announced, "I'm calling him Alexander the Great."

"Pretty big name for a little guy," Dad said. "How about Al?"

I walked Alex three times a day because he was thrilled to go out. As he grew, he walked me as he sniffed the news. On weekends, Alex rode in my bike basket to the golf course. While I collected stray balls, he hunted for ground squirrels.

The nine-hole golf course was modest and weather beaten, like the town. My dad, and half of Clarksburg, worked at the John Deere factory. My favorite hangout, the Carnegie Library, didn't allow dogs, so I didn't visit there much anymore.

I owed some of my freedom that summer to Alex. One evening, I overheard my parents in the backyard, sipping beer.

"About time you admitted I was right," Dad said.

"About what?"

"That dog. He's been good for Nan. He's got her on the go day and night."

"He does, but I don't know that's such a good thing. I'd just as soon she didn't run all over town by herself."

"But she's not by herself. She's got the dog. And she hasn't got her head stuck in a book all the time like she used to."

"At least she was safe at the library. I don't know where she is sometimes."

"This isn't Chicago, Alice. She couldn't get lost in this town if she tried."

"I don't mean lost."

The cushion on the folding chair sighed. By the time the screen door screeched open, I was headed upstairs, Alex bounding ahead of me.

As an only child, I was used to entertaining myself, and most kids in my neighborhood were several years older or younger, so Alex became my constant companion. One humid July morning, we went down by the river to pick blackberries. I considered leaving Alex home; he'd just collect burrs. But Mom would put him in the backyard and he preferred investigating the larger world.

The outer bushes of the wild blackberry patch, those facing the road, were picked over. Only crouching or stretching overhead yielded the ripe berries. That prospect lured me into the thicket. Brambles plucked at me and grasshoppers leapt as I ventured further. When I heard a rustle underfoot—a snake? Rats? I climbed a boulder. Birds had nibbled the fruit atop the bushes. Hot air vibrated like a cloud of gnats, and a breeze off the river tickled the leaves. Soon, I was practically dizzy from the berries' fragrance, eating one for every three in the bucket. The taste made up for the accompanying spider webs and winged bugs, powdery gray like moths.

The bucket was half full when Alex started barking, probably at other kids picking berries—the bushes stretched about 50 yards along the riverbank. But Alex sounded upset. With his leash tied around a butternut tree trunk, he could nose around but not reach the road. He stood, barking with his whole body, squared off against a man trying to free his pants leg from briars. When he straightened up, a thick vine hooked itself to his shirt. "Damnation."

I almost laughed. Then he saw me. "Call off your dog, little missy."

I didn't like being called that, but he smiled in a way—wide with dimples—that made you smile back. To quiet Alex, I rubbed his chest. "What a good, smart boy," I said. He stopped barking but trembled.

"What are you doing?" I asked the man.

"Picking berries, same as you," he said, as he finished freeing himself from the thorny canes. His shadow fell on me.

"Where's your bucket?"

"Oh, I'm not collecting any," he said. "Just eating 'em for breakfast."

Maybe he was one of the hobos I'd heard about who passed through on the freight train; I was sorry that Alex had bothered him.

"At Svenhard's bakery, you can get day-old rolls half price."

"Is that a fact? I could eat a jelly donut or three or four."

Then he plucked two berries and popped them in his mouth, and I noticed his fingertips weren't purple like mine. I also noticed that his jeans were unzipped. I backed up.

"Sure tasty," the man said and smiled again.

I nodded and untied Alex, who was sitting now. I jerked his leash. "C'mon."

The man reached for a cluster of berries overhead. He grabbed one berry, and as he pulled it off the cluster snapped back up. He stood on tiptoe to reach again. "Tantalizing. The best are always out of reach."

"Those are for the birds." I tugged at Alex.

"You know about old Tantalus, don't you?"

I shook my head.

"He was a king back in the days of the ancient Greeks. Got sent to Hades—hell—and his punishment was to stand in a pool of water with a bunch of fruit hanging off a branch above him. If he tried to eat the fruit, the wind moved it out of his reach. If he tried to drink, the water level dropped. So he was surrounded by plenty but had to do without. Forever."

What had Tantalus done to be punished? I was afraid to ask.

"Anyhow, that's where we get tantalize," he said, drawing out the last word. A crow caught Alex's interest, and as he stood, I pulled him away.

"Bye," the man said. I felt him watching me head for my bike.

Alex ran alongside me; I pedaled fast for about a mile and stopped at a gas station. Alex lapped water from a Dixie cup I filled and refilled. In years past, I'd picked berries at that same spot without Alex. What if that man had snuck up on me alone? With the quarter in my pocket—Mom said always carry one for the phone—I got cheese crackers with peanut butter from the vending machine for Alex.

When Mom poured the fruit into a colander, she said, "This isn't enough to make jam. Why didn't you pick more?"

"I got hot," I said. I didn't want to mention the man. If I did, she'd tell me to stay away from there, not go off by myself. And nothing had happened, really. I'd sensed he was lying. Adults and kids lie to each other all the time. His lie was the kind without good intentions. Mine was harmless. "It's your fault, making me wear these long sleeves and pants."

"I didn't want you getting all scratched up." She pulled a leaf from my hair. "I can make a pie with these. But blackberry jam is your father's favorite."

"I'll get more tomorrow," I said.

"Tomorrow's Saturday. We're going to the lake this weekend, remember?"

"OK, I'll get berries Monday." I had forgotten my plans to teach Alex how to swim. Meanwhile, I wanted to find out about this Tantalus guy. I didn't want to ask my mother; she'd want to know why I was asking. I looked in our encyclopedia—nothing—and in the dictionary, which confirmed the origin of tantalize. It did seem an awful predicament, being up to your neck in water but unable to drink, fruit dangling just out of reach. What had Tantalus done?

After lunch I rode over to the library. I asked the librarian, "Can you tell me about Tantalus?"

"Tantalus? Is that an author's name or a book title?"

"I think he lived in ancient Greece." Soon we were in the reference section thumbing through a thick book of mythology. It said Tantalus killed and cooked his son and served him to the gods, but it didn't say why. Once the gods figured out what had happened, they restored life to the boy, but hauled Tantalus down to Hades. Then everyone in his family suffered for several generations. How come the blackberry man knew this story? I thought only nice people were smart.

At the lake, swimming lessons were unnecessary—Alex darted in the water with glee. I caught a trout big enough to keep and entertained Alex by capturing fireflies in a mayonnaise jar while also collecting mosquito bites.

The man at the berry patch faded from my thoughts, like the scratches on my hands, until Monday morning, when Mom reminded me about the jam. I didn't want to return, even with Alex. He could protect me or at least

warn me, but I didn't want him to get hurt. I figured the blackberry man was long gone and remembered the way the house smelled when jam cooked.

"Go on, Nan. It's not so hot yet. I can make the jam this afternoon."

So off we went, Alex loping along. I parked my bike at the south end of the bushes, as far as possible from where I'd been Friday. Soon mud covered my Keds and sweat trickled around my ribs. Ripe berries were scarce at this spot. Like a flock of crows, weekend pickers had landed here. I stooped, thorns snagging my fingers, to grasp plump, dark berries, the ones that practically fell off. The bucket held a few pints when Alex rushed up. His tail beat against my legs.

I patted between his ears. "It's too hot to get worked up over a squirrel."

He ran off and pulled against his leash so that the bushes shook. Then he came back, pleading with his eyes. He dashed off again and started howling. I dropped the bucket and ran after him. To keep him from choking, I unsnapped the leash. He bounded over to a log and started digging under it. He soon had a softball in his mouth and dropped it at my feet, but not to play fetch. Alex returned to the log, frantic, scooping a hole in the sandy soil. He wrestled something out with his teeth and brought it to me. A baseball glove. On the palm were the initials T. Q. written in black Magic Marker. Tommy Quinn. The youngest Quinn, he lived several blocks from me. A third grader. His sister and I were the same age, but had never been friends. Why would Tommy have buried his ball and glove? Alex remained revved up, so I put them in my bike basket and headed home.

On my way, I stopped at Tommy's house. Mr. Quinn answered the door, which seemed odd for a Monday morning. Before I could say anything, he grabbed the glove from my hands. "Where'd you get this?"

When I learned Tommy was missing, I told Mr. Quinn about the stranger in the berry patch Friday. He called the police. I described the man and answered their questions. And I had to tell my parents.

"Oh, Nan. Why didn't you say something about him on Friday?" Mom asked.

Through my tears I said, "I don't know," but I did.

By Wednesday, the police had located the blackberry man. He was in Indiana. I identified him from a Pola-

Q: Any advice to new writers hoping to enter the field?

A: The best possible advice I can give to any aspiring writer is to read, read, read, and analyze, and write, write, write. Writing is a craft, and any craft is improved with practice. But most importantly is to read the most successful of the kind of works you would yourself like to write: So, if you want to be, for instance, a crime thriller writer, read the blockbusters of the past fifty years. Analyze them, literally deconstruct them and try to figure out what made them so popular. This is what I did when I started out. I took the books I most admired, the ones I most wished I had written, and literally read them until I knew them inside out.

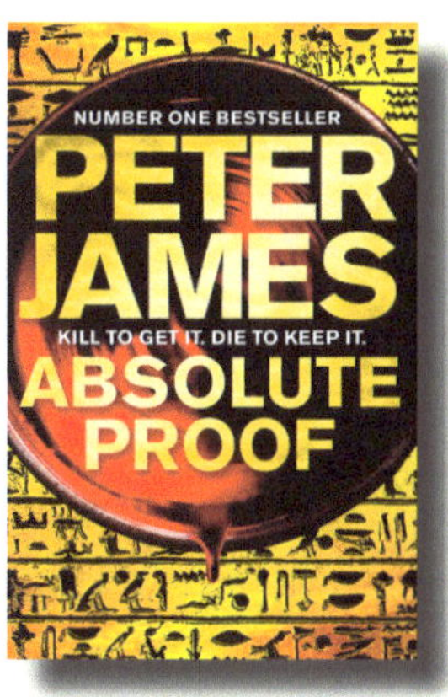

Peter James "Absolute Proof" is due to be released October, 2018. A standalone book not in the crime genre, it focuses on what could happen were someone of credibility to claim to have an absolute proof for the existence of God.

Our thanks to Peter for taking the time for this interview.

Here are his Social Media links:
YouTube channel: www.peterjames.com/YouTube
•Website: www.peterjames.com
•Facebook: http://www.facebook.com/peterjames.roygrace
•Twitter: http://twitter.com/peterjamesuk
•Instagram: https://instagram.com/peterjamesuk
•Instagram Pets: https://instagram.com/peterjamesukpets
•Amazon Author Page: http://www.amazon.com/Peter-James/e/B000APS7L4

Photo credit page 4: Lara James

by Charles Hitchcock

I slammed the door shut behind me and stood there shaking. Every muscle in my body was jerking uncontrollably as beads of sweat ran down the wrinkles on my face, dripping off my chin. I wondered if the California heat had finally got to me. I fumbled for my cigarettes, but they dropped to the floor. I kicked the box and they scattered. I must be wrong, I told myself. The man I just left could not have been George Edwards. Not after spending 20 years in prison. I couldn't be that lucky.

I reached down and managed to get hold of one of the cigarettes, lit it and sat down of the edge the big steel bed. The springs groaned with age.

I looked around the dingy one-room shack with broken windows and torn shades. A shaft of sunlight came through a hole in the roof, and I could smell the dust that filtered through it.

I wasn't like this 20 years ago. Back in those days I was a young geologist headed for success. A twisted smile formed on my mouth and ended in a curse because it split my parched lip. I went places okay— San Quentin.

My wife left me and took our son with her. I couldn't blame her. What woman would want a murderer for a husband. Partly, she left for the sake of our child. No, I couldn't blame her. I only hope they find some happiness that I could not give them. Edwards, now he is to blame. The only thing left to live for now is to watch him die. When Edwards dies, my tortured brain will find peace.

Thinking of Edwards gave me a bad taste in my mouth. My stomach tightened, and I stamped the butt out on the floor.

Prison does something to a man. After a while, you get through the days okay, but the nights you just lie on your bunk and think. You think about home and tears well up in your eyes. Then, after a short while, you get tough. Tough from the hard labor you're forced to work during the day. Tough inside from the thoughts that come with the night.

For years I dreamed of the day I would see Edwards again. I knew he wasn't dead, but until today, I couldn't prove it. Now I could. Edwards was alive. Five minutes ago he stood right there in front of me, his fat belly protruding over his belt. Now he was the big boss of the oil field. He hadn't changed much.; less hair on his head and maybe a little fatter. He stood there in his white suit and fifty-cent cigar stuck in his thick overgrown lips as he barked orders. His stubby fingers pointed out the work that still had to be done. He saw me, but after all these years, didn't recognize me. No surprise, I wasn't the same man that went to jail— because of him. Over half my life wasted, because of him.

My heart pumped harder, the black-oil of hate spilling into my brain and draining into every nerve and muscle. I stood up and grabbed the bottle of bourbon off the dresser. Frowning at the image in the mirror, I poured myself a drink. There was nothing left of me except a soul searching for revenge.

I gulped down the bourbon and poured another. I had to think. One drink followed another and soon the bottle was nearing empty. I decided, after all these years, I could wait a little longer. I lay down and let a plan run through my mind.

When I awoke I was shivering. The desert air was always cool at night. Now was time for action. Edwards would be alone, probably asleep by now. This is what I had waited for. My heart pumped with excitement. It pounded and my breath came hard. I pulled my .38 revolver out of the drawer and lovingly, ran my hands over it. Then I stuck it in my belt.

I headed out for the highway. There was an all-night joint called "Ernie's" and the bartender was more than happy to give me Edwards' address in exchange for a five-dollar bill.

Silver City was only 12 miles from the joint. It was a small town, and it wouldn't take me long to find the address.

An old car was parked outside Ernie's place and the owner had been fool enough to leave the keys in it. Just what I needed. I slid under the wheel, started her up, and raced off down the highway. Through the rear view mirror I could see that no one had followed me. Good. By the time I was through with the car the owner wouldn't want it back, anyway.

I swung into a gas station and bought a gallon of gas which I filled into a jug in the back seat. The attendant thanked me and gave me directions for the address I wanted.

A few minutes later I was there. I got out and held back a laugh as I soaked the inside of the car with the gasoline.

There weren't any lights on in the house, but I rang the doorbell anyway, until I heard the sound of heavy footsteps inside. I took a deep breath and pulled the .38 out of my belt. The inside lights came on and then the front door opened.

I slammed the .38 across that big blubbering mouth before it could make a sound. Edwards fell to the floor. I kicked the door shut behind me. He looked ridiculous; A big glob of blubber with hairy legs sticking out from under a big, blue house-robe. They has a look of amazement on his face as he wiped at the blood trickling out of his mouth with the back of his hand.

I grabbed a handful of what hair he had left on his head and pulled him into a sitting position. Now he looked scared. He had a right to be scared. He was going to die, but not before knowing why. I put my face down next to his. "Remember me, Edwards"?

"Who—who are you"? he asked. The fright in his eyes turned to terror. There was a quiver in his voice.

"Don't you know the man who went to prison for killing you?" I asked as I moved closer.

"No, you cant be... You're not...?"

"Yeah, I'm Joe Barton. Take a good look. This is what prison does to a man".

"Look Joe, I'll make it up to you. Anything you want. Just name it," he whimpered.

"No, Edwards, you're not getting off. I was afraid you might have already died and I would be cheated out of my revenge. But you're alive and I haven't been cheated. Watching you die is the moment I've dreamed of".

He licked his lips but his tongue was dry. He was really scared now. He couldn't speak. He just sat there gasping for air. Every muscle in his massive bulk either twitched or was paralyzed. This is exactly what I wanted. He could sit there and think about his death.

"Edwards, I know you can hear me so listen closely and think about what I say. Think back to the days when we were both young. You were green-eyed with jealousy of my ambition and rapid success, but you fixed all that and made a fortune for yourself at the same time. Remember Edwards?" I asked as I pressed the .38 between his eyes.

I thought he would faint, for a moment, but he just nodded weakly.

"Good, then you remember the night when you robbed the Shafer Oil Company? You were seen so you had to take care of that. You mailed a confession to the police but to get me, you told them I was the brains behind the robbery. Then you stole my car. The rest I'm not too sure about. Was it a drunk or a bum that just happened to be handy that you could switch clothes and ID with? No Matter! When the police found my car it had been burned and the body couldn't be recognized. You were smart Edwards. The cops did think it was your body in the car when they found pieces of your ring and your watch, along with other things belonging to you. They nailed me for the killing because it was my car. They dropped the charges of robbery against me because of lack of evidence, but I was stuck with the murder rap that got me a life sentence with parole after 20 years. Think about it Edwards. Think like I did. You didn't figure on ever seeing me again, did you? Well finally I got lucky. I wasn't able to land a good job because of being an ex-con but I did get a job as a roughneck with this dinky operation. This afternoon when I saw you in the oil field I was barely able to control myself. But, after years of waiting, patience becomes a habit. I went home and waited for tonight, and now its here Edwards. Your time is up. How does it feel to know you're about to die"?

Edwards had a look of disbelief in his eyes, they were huge now and looked like the were about to pop out of their sockets. It was too much for him to take in all at once. I stood up and motioned for to get up.

He started for his feet and with a huge surge of power suddenly knocked me out of his way. My .38 fell to the floor and Edwards pounced on it. We were both on our feet at the same time grasping for the gun, but he had it. His eyes narrowed to thin slits. I could see what he was going to do, and there wasn't a thing I could do about it, but I wasn't going to quit now. Not after coming so close to getting him. I wasn't going to let him get away now.

I moved closer and could see his finger tighten on the trigger. There was a brilliant flash, but I didn't hear anything. Something had knocked me backwards and my legs wouldn't support my body. I fell to the floor. My

hand was clutching my abdomen and when I took it away it was a wet crimson. I looked up at Edwards. He had won, again. I knew I was dying and would be helpless to do anything else. Even to the death, Edwards was going to have the last laugh.

For a moment, he just stood there looking back at me. He saw the red blood pulsing out of my stomach, and looked like he was going to puke. I hoped he would. His hands dropped to his side and began to tremble. The gun hung loosely around his stubby forefinger. He couldn't take anymore. He whirled and bolted outside. The gun slipped off his finger and fell in the open doorway.

The gun wasn't far away, but I doubted if I could make it in time. I clawed at the floor and inched toward it. I could feel the clouds gathering in my brain. It wouldn't be long. My belly was soggy with blood. I heard the faint sound of a car starting up outside. I had to make it. I strained every muscle in a last attempt to reach the gun. Then my hand closed around it. I lay in the doorway laughing. He was in the car I had stolen and now had the motor running.

I could have laughed my damn-fool head off. Things were beginning to haze in my mind. I fired-off the remaining shells into the car. A spark ignited the gasoline-soaked automobile and it burst into flame. I could see Edwards' frenzied efforts as he realized what was happening. Finally, the brilliance of the fire dimmed in my eyes, but I didn't care anymore. All I could do was just lay there and laugh.

ABOUT THE AUTHOR:

Charles (Charlie) Hitchcock was born in Hooker Oklahoma in 1931. Hooker was in ground-zero of The Dust Bowl in the 30s and 40s. Charlie always had an active inquisitive mind that helped him throughout his life and enabled him to escape the Oklahoma Prairie and build a life in Southern California.

While in the Air Force in 1952, Charlie caught the writing bug, and he wrote several short stories to see if he could pen a story as well as his favorite author, Mickey Spillane. Those who read his stories encouraged him to continue, but as is with most folks, living life and trying to earn a living took priority. He did periodically return to writing and wrote a handful of great songs and short stories.

Charlie passed away June 2006. His son, Cliff, has assembled his work for an upcoming book. This is one of the stories.

Story Photo credits: Oleg Vydyborets & Miroslav Benedal123RF.com

Books 'N Pieces Magazine is published 6 times a year by Alt Publishing, P.O. Box 51, Emmett, Idaho.

All questions should be directed to info@booksnpieces.com. Authors, if you would like to be interviewed for this publication, please email us with your bio, links and any relevant information. If you wish to submit short stories or other materia, you may do so from our Website listed above.

You may also follow us on Facebook: www.FB.com/BandPMagazine or Twitter: www.twitter.com/BooksNPiecesMag

BIG WORDS

Some of these are just fun to know, while others may prove to be useful in your writing. If you have some words to share, email them to info@ booksnpieces.com

PUNNET (n): a small container or basket for fruit *(Aust/British)*

ISOPOLITY (n): equal rights of citizenship: mutual political rights

EPIGONE (n): an undistinguished imitator: successor of an important writer.

TUMMLER (n): a prankish, mischievous man : A male entertainer

GARBOLOGY (n): the study of discarded materials in order to learn social or cultural patterns.

COEVAL (adj): of the same age : equally old.

FLEXITARIAN (n): a person whose diet is mostly vegetarian or who mixes it up with fish.

TUROPHILE (n): a lover of cheese.

SENNIGHT (n): a week (anachronistic)

CRAIC (n): Fun and entertaining, related to conversing and communications.

WRITERS ON THE EDGE!

interview

LiveStream, YouTube Podcast For Authors, By Authors, Reaches Large, Global Fanbase

Q: The Writers' Edge started last year, and features a wide range of guests from newbie and Indie authors, thru New York Times bestselling authors. What was the genesis of the idea behind this show and how has audience (YouTube) reaction been?

A: Christie (Stratos) was given The Writer's Edge (what a nice gift!) by fellow author Joshua Robertson a year ago, and the idea has always been to discuss writing in all aspects - advice for writing holiday-based books, what self-publishing vs. traditional publishing looks like, balancing writing with your job and life, and so much more. Mickey (Mikkelson) came on-board recently, and at that point we added one-on-one interviews to our livestream panel discussions.

Now we're on every second and fourth Thursday at 9 p.m. EST. We always keep our eyes out for experts, people with a lot of experience or even varied experience depending on the topic, so that we have a diverse and helpful discussion. The reaction has been very positive, with viewers who attend every livestream, and ask questions, and new viewers networking with our consistent ones. It's amazing to watch those connections form. In reality, our show is meant to give exposure to any one who is in the literary industry and that is really how we want to be identified and related with!

Q: How far reaching is your audience, and do you find responses vary based on the country of the viewer (not unlike British and American humor are different)?

A: Our largest viewership is in America, but we always have plenty of viewers in Canada, Mexico, the UK, France, Germany, Australia, and even India! Neither of us has noticed a difference in response because of culture, but most who are vocal during the chat either ask questions, share their own ideas, or just have a nice conversation. As for reach, we are also looking to expand our reach and we will always tweak *and adjust when something is working.*

Q: What sort of advance prep is required to put on an Internet show, and to what degree is it scripted versus free-flowing?

A: The first step is coming up with the topic, something that will be appealing and helpful. Then we find guests who suit the topic. Once those preliminary steps are completed, Christie develops the questions and sends them to the participants, although live questions from viewers are encouraged too. Nothing is scripted, but the panelists do know about the set ques-

tions ahead of time. We create a Facebook event, create a YouTube event, and voila! A show is ready to go live.

Q: Where would you like to see the progress of the show headed in the future?

A: We have already had some sponsorships, but we're looking to gain further sponsorships to help bring us to a larger audience. At this time, sponsorships are extremely affordable and earn the sponsor air time with a wonderful audience of engaged writers. We've already expanded the show to be twice per month instead of just once, and now that we have both panel discussion and interview style shows, we are looking to expand the types of guests we have beyond (but still including) authors. We're looking at reviewers, publicists, booktubers, publishers, and more, anything that is going to create interest and exhibit entertaining and dynamic episodes.

Q: How do you select your guests?

A: Sometimes we already know authors who are perfect for the show, sometimes we search for authors who have experience and offer diverse viewpoints. On our "Variety is the Spice of Writing Romance" panel, we had authors who write romantic comedy, military romance, romantic suspense, contemporary romance - a great variety of subgenres, both with publishers and self-published. Our goal is the ensure that everyone always has something to add, even if it's to disagree and share very different experiences. Everything is helpful when it comes to sharing writing, marketing, and publishing advice. In the past, we have even had prolific writers and not yet published writers on the show to share their own writing advice and experiences; each one had extremely relatable things to say.

Q: Does this format enhance sales for authors, if you know?

A: We've certainly gotten feedback that it can enhance their social media following, but we don't have information about their sales. The other aspect to think about is that guests are accountable to share the feed as well. Like any media vehicle, it will only be effective if everyone works together to get the word out about their episode. Its like any other marketing scheme, more views should equal more sales long term!

Watch all the episode of The Writer's Edge at https://www.youtube.com/channel/UCrFrRVtl0YyaR8NEYAdZ24w

WRITER GUIDELINES

So you'd like to submit your short story to Books 'N Pieces Magazine? We'd love to see it. Our guidelines are simple:

•Have a great story. Don't tell a sliver of a story, don't tease a story (especially if you are using the short story to promote a novel), no excerpts (unless otherwise approved), and no stolen work.

•Your story MUST HAVE a beginning, middle and end, to what you are trying to convey; the character must CHANGE throughout the story.

•Show DON'T tell. Narration is all well and good if it serves a purpose. Readers want to SEE the story.

•Don't get creative with post dialog attributes—he said, she said, is just fine. You don't need, "This stinks," he spat. Unless he really spits, don't say it. "I don't like the curtains," she said leisurely. Unless it took her a very long and comfortable time, do not use that word.

•Avoid stupid words that do not exist, are overused, or misused:

And while "he said," and "she said," are all fine, when you have two people talking, you should be able to quickly figure out who is talking. Just use that "said" the first time and intermittently, but not after every sentence."

Proper dialog format is as follows: "I really like the curtains," he said. It is NOT, "I really like the curtains!" He said. By the way, exclamation marks are for exclaiming—you know, vibrantly emphatic!!!!!

Please ~~prood~~ proof your work before you submit it. If you care that little about your work to submit it without having gone through it, what response are you expecting from me? Excellent proofing methods include reading it aloud, having someone read it to you, record it and play it back. You will be amazed at the mistakes you find.

Please avoid ALL CAPS. IT LOOKS LIKE YOU ARE SCREAMING AND EVEN IF YOUR CHARACTER IS SCREAMING IT SHOULD BE IN lower case.

IMPORTANT: Please make sure that any quotations, citations, selections from other materials you use, are not copyrighted, or that you own the copyright, or have written permission to use it. While you are allowed "fair use" selections, you need to be familiar with the laws that protect these works. When in

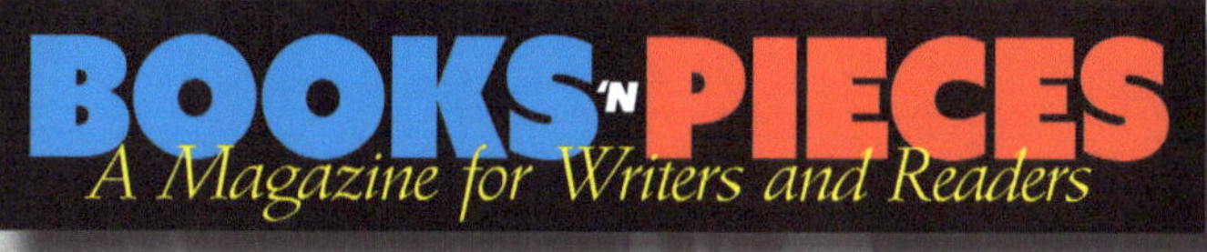

doubt, ask.

Please do not submit formatted work. Text is best. Your fancy font that made you feel good, will only irritate me as I have to strip it back to text before I use it. No offense.

Should your work be accepted for publication, it will pass through an editing process. While we endeavor to retain your work as closely as possible, editing may require us to adjust your work for reader clarity, in addition to grammatical corrections. We may elect to change the title of your work, however we will ask you first and work with you.

TIPS: Learn how your writing can be powerful. Below are two links to short stories that you should read. Each offers a different style and you can use them as an example of what makes a powerful story.

• Here is a link to a short story by Ernest Hemingway*. It is an excellent example of the power of a short story, without being overt in explanation. I hope you will find them useful.

Http://bit.ly/HemingwayHills

• Another excellent short story* "Mrs. Dutta Writes a Letter" is available Online to read as well. Http://bit.ly/MrsDuttaWrites

And finally, here is a link to a FREE novel by bestselling author, Mike Wells. I suggest you read the PROLOGUE so you can see how he has turned the first five pages into a powerhouse piece of writing. https://bit.ly/1uXO2og

*Note: Books 'N Pieces Magazine has no affiliation with the above listed Websites. The links are provided as a courtesy only.

If you have other questions, please contact info@Booksnpieces.com and include B&P in the subject line.

PAYMENT

Payment is a flat rate of US$100 for previously unpublished stories over 1000 words with no limit to length, and a flat rate US$50 if your story has been published elsewhere, or is under 1000 words.

Payment will be made upon acceptance (generally within a few weeks of receipt). We like PayPal, however can also send you a check (cheque for those of you overseas) or other mutually agreeable method.

We pay US$25 for poems we accept, regardless of length.

We claim only the right to publish your work in the magazine (within 4 months), and also on the magazine's website. All other rights remain with the author.

Please SUBMIT from the Website www.BooksNPieces.com Select the SUBMIT menu option. Allow 2-4 weeks to hear back.

I look forward to reading your submissions.

NOTHING TO FEAR

by Jim Hasse

It was a chest crushing bearhug.

My arms were pinned to my sides. I was spun around, and now faced a madman. His teeth were bared, and he was growling. His face was red, and his eyes bulged.

He blurted out in a hoarse whisper, "You fuckin' narc, you're dead."

There was a large knife in his right hand, raised above his head. As he attacked toward my neck I grunted, struggled, and pulled my left arm free.

The knife and my forearm met about two inches from my neck. I didn't even feel the pain. I was breathing hard, and my mind was racing. The blade of the knife was momentarily stuck in the bone of my forearm, about six inches from my wrist.

I bucked and kicked and tried to head-butt this crazy man. The knife was pulled free, and again swiped at my throat. This time I pulled back and pivoted sideways as the blade clipped my left shoulder. I was fighting for my life.

My Mauser .380 automatic was wedged in the back of my jeans, next to my sweaty skin. As I fended off the attacker with my left hand and kicked for his groin with my right leg, I managed to get my right hand under my t-shirt and wrap my hand around the pistol grips.

The man holding me from behind threw his left arm around my neck and started to choke me. As I freed my pistol from the waistband of my jeans, my attacker plunged the knife into the middle of my belly.

It was a hard punch to the gut. I struggled and pulled away as he tried to twist the knife. I raised the pistol, and the man behind me wrestled it out of my hand, as we all fell to the ground.

While I tried to poke my fingers into the attacker's eyes, I felt the pistol pressed hard against the back of my head. I snapped my head forward just as the gun discharged. A searing pain pierced the back of my scalp, followed by a ringing in my ears.

A physical power that I did not know I possessed flowed through me and I threw the forward attacker off and rolled over, wrenching my pistol out of the other man's hand. The attackers scrambled to their feet and stumbled away.

I was now on my knees, panting for breath. Sweat was dripping into my eyes and my hands were slippery with blood.

I pointed my gun toward their fleeing backs and fired three rounds in succession. I fell forward onto my elbows and it felt as though I was about to black out. I looked up, and all I could see were the woods about 20 yards away.

I pushed up onto my knees and fired three more rounds into the woods. The world turned dark as I collapsed face-first onto the dusty ground.

My portable radio crackled, and I heard my partner, Mike Higgins, yelling my name. "Gabhann, where are you? Gabhann, Gabhann, where are you?"

I struggled to get to my feet and reached for my radio that was sitting on the roof of my undercover vehicle. I keyed the mic, "Officer down, officer down. Two zero, one zero, I'm by the car. I'm by the car."

I could now hear the sound of running and Mike yelling, "I'm coming, I'm coming."

I slid down the side of the Camaro and tried to think. Was this real? I couldn't feel any pain. I felt the back of my head and could feel a bloody, mushy spot with a chunk of scalp missing.

I felt my stomach area and it was tender to the touch. I was shaking and felt dizzy.

Mike rounded the corner and slid into a kneeling position to my left.

"Oh my God! Have you been shot? Let me see! Let me see! Where is it?"

"Two white males, big, mid 30's, both denim jackets, dark jeans. Both had big beards. Dirty blond hair. Guy in front had a gap between his front teeth."

"Are you shot?"

"Just grazed, in the back of the head. I think I'm okay. I was stabbed here," I said as I placed my hand over my belly. "I think that's the worst of it." I looked at the bloody palm of my hand. "I feel disoriented. I'm bleeding pretty heavily."

"Madison County, this is Meg two zero. Officer down. Officer down. Meg one zero needs an ambulance for a serious stab wound. We are at MRF in the north lot. I'll put a red flasher on top of our unmarked car."

"Roger Meg, two zero. Ambulance dispatched. Give me a description of the..." That was the last I heard.

The next sound was chopper blades. Dust was blowing everywhere. It was like a violent windstorm. Was I in Vietnam? This was all too familiar. God, let this be a flashback, a nightmare. My left forearm was throbbing, I had a blinding headache, and I could feel blood running down into my crotch. My jeans were soaked in a sticky mess.

There was now a medic on my right side. He had cut my t-shirt open down the front and was putting a compress bandage over my wound.

Mike leaned down and said, "We're loading you in the chopper for a short flight. Detective Martin from Madison County, Bill Martin, is riding over with you. He wants as much information as possible. Give him all the details. We've got to catch these guys. A sheriff's patrol car saw two bikers come off a nature trail and head toward the freeway. They lost them as they headed west toward East St. Louis."

"I feel so tired. Why can't we talk at the hospital? I just want to sleep. Just want to sleep. Let me rest."

"No Ted, you can't sleep. You must be alert. You're in bad shape. You've lost a lot of blood. I don't want to scare you, but they need as much information as possible just in case you don't make it. That's why Martin is flying with you."

I gave a weak wave to Mike as we lifted off. The helicopter ride was a loud, mind-numbing blur. Bill Martin and I tried to talk, but we had trouble hearing each other. Although the air was cold, I was sweating profusely. I was having trouble breathing, and I could feel panic setting in. I could see the bloody gauze bandage on my forearm, and I was shaking all over. Blood was soaking through the bandage on my abdomen.

Detective Martin had a pad and pen in his hands and asked me what the attackers looked like. I knew I was repeating much of what I had told Mike earlier. It was necessary to yell to be heard, "Two big white guys. One taller than the other. Both had beards. I could smell alcohol on them. The guy in front had a gap in his teeth. You know, in his front teeth. I just can't remember everything. Can I have something for pain?"

Martin turned sideways and said something to a medic just behind him. The medic smiled as he leaned over me and shook his head in the negative and said, "Sorry man. You've got a head wound. Can't give you anything. Be at the hospital soon." He then asked my blood type.

The pitch of the rotor was changing, and I could feel the chopper descending. There was a bounce of the skids touching down. A bolt of pain shot through my head. There was lots of noise and confusion as my stretcher was offloaded onto a gurney.

As the gurney was moved, the pain in my abdomen radiated outward and up into my chest. I felt like I was going to vomit and the thought of that scared me. "God, make the pain stop." The noise of the helicopter receded behind me and I could hear excited voices. I heard someone say, "Yeah, he's a cop. An undercover state narcotics agent. Grazing gunshot to the back of the head and stab wound in the center of abdomen. Pretty serious."

A tall man in a white coat said something to me that I didn't understand. He had the bearing of a doctor. I closed my eyes and shook my head from side to side, "Help me get through this. I'm really hurting."

It made me more nervous that everyone was so serious and I heard the medic that had been on the helicopter say, "His blood pressure kept dropping. Looks like serious internal bleeding to me." It seemed like a lot of bad news.

Then there was this smiling face. An attractive woman, just a little older than me, probably around 35. She was tall and had long blonde hair. She was walking beside me. She must have been a nurse. She was so calm and focused. She took my right hand into her hands and gently squeezed. It was a feeling of warmth and assurance. She whispered, "You have nothing fear."

I suddenly felt calm, even relaxed. All of the excitement seemed to subside, and it was peaceful. The tall man, who had a stethoscope around his neck leaned closer as he walked along beside me, "Have you had anything to drink?

"No, I was working. We were about to do a buy-bust, a big case, I wasn't drinking!"

"No, I mean water or coffee, not alcohol. We need to prep you for surgery. I need to know if you have any liquid in your stomach. You could aspirate."

"No. I'm really dry, really thirsty."

The double doors to the emergency room slid open with a whoosh, and I was wheeled into a small room with drapes for privacy. There were four or five medical personnel gathered around me.

"Pain, really painful, I need something. I need it now."

The man I had spoken to earlier, who had just been called Dr. Brand, examined the back of my head, as a technician inserted a needle into a vein on the inside of my right forearm and on the top of my hand. Dr. Brand nodded to the technician and said, "Give him max Demerol."

On the ride over I had been asked what my blood type was. They had called ahead to the emergency room and had units of O-positive waiting for me. There was now a bag of blood hanging from a rod above my head.

I heard the doctor say to Detective Martin, "No. You can't talk to him now. We're prepping him for surgery. We've got to go."

The blonde nurse leaned over me.

She had a soft, caring smile. I looked at her name tag. The white letters etched into the black background said, Gabhann. What? That's my name. She wasn't a relative. Other than family I had never met another Gabhann.

I said, "Gabhann? That's my name! It's an unusual name. Gabhann, really?"

She nodded and said, "There are a few of us around. We need to stick together," and she winked.

She gently touch my forehead and I felt at peace. I felt strong and wasn't afraid anymore. I guess the Demerol was kicking in.

The attendants stripped off the remainder of my t-shirt and my jeans, socks and shoes. They cleaned me up and placed a sheet over me that covered the lower part of my body.

I looked around for nurse Gabhann, but she wasn't in the room. I asked the doctor, "Where is the nurse?"

"I don't know. We need to go now. We're going to get you all fixed up."

As we moved into the elevator I became very sleepy. We moved up three floors and then down the hallway to the surgery center.

I noticed that blood from my stomach wound was soaking through the white sheet. The crimson color was spreading. Technicians began to attach wires leading to the monitors and a blood pressure cuff on my upper right arm. I was in a relaxed twilight, but was aware of what was going on. Dr. Brand had scrubbed and entered the room.

A technician said, "Blood pressure is hypotensive, 85 over 49. Heart rate is 135."

Standing just behind him was my nurse, my namesake. She was radiant. She was glowing. She didn't have a face mask or scrubs on. No one seemed to notice her. She moved over to my left shoulder, gently smoothed my hair, and said, "Remember, you have nothing to fear."

I could feel the anxiety and rushed movements of those around me, but I was at peace and was actually happy. Warmth flow through my veins, and I was completely relaxed. The doctor took a deep breath and began an incision adjacent to my puncture wound. As he opened me up he said, "The vein to the spleen has been severed. I've got to clamp it off."

He worked quickly, with an intense focus. Blood continued to flow from the incision. Dr. Brand mumbled, "Damn, I can't get to it."

As one bag of blood emptied it was

replaced by a second. Suddenly there was a loud and steady noise coming from the heart monitor. An alarm sounded. As the doctor continued to try to clamp off the bleeding vein, another alarm sounded. I was flatlining.

I wasn't excited and seemed detached from it all. I looked over at my nurse. She had a soft, friendly smile. She nodded at me and mouthed, "It's okay. It's okay." I smiled and nodded back. She was so encouraging, and I loved it.

Dr. Brand lifted a set of defibrillation paddles from a cart and placed them on each side of my chest. "Clear," he said. My body arched upward and bounced on the table. The sound of the flatline and the other alarms continued to shout their ominous warnings.

Dr. Brand tried again, and this time I made eye contact with my nurse. She seemed calm and patient. She placed her palms together and held them in front of her heart in a prayer position.

Why were all these people so excited? It wasn't the end of anything; it felt like the beginning. The alarms were silenced. The medical staff stood quietly together.

Dr. Brand shook his head and looked defeated. They all just stared at my body. Then they slowly walked out of the room.

Although they were gone I didn't feel alone. I just rested peacefully for a few minutes and then my nurse was back by my side.

She took my hands in hers. I had never felt so unconditionally loved - not a worry in the world. She gently embraced me and together, we drifted off to sleep.

ABOUT THE AUTHOR:

Jim Hasse writes about intriguing, poignant, and sometimes humorous experiences influenced by his time in Vietnam as sergeant in Special Forces and in his 26-years in law enforcement. He was a criminal investigator, an undercover narcotics detective, and a U.S. Postal Inspector. Earning a master's in counseling, he became a drug and alcohol rehabilitation instructor. Hasse is a member of the California Writers Club and the Concord Veterans Writers Group. He lives in the San Francisco Bay Area with his wife, Carol..

Photo Credit: Jaromír Chalabala & 9nong l123rf.com

The Woman in Cabin 10

The Woman in Cabin 10 by Ruth Ware (2017, Gallery/Scout Press; Reprint edition, paperback, 384 pages $9.80) is the perfect book for edge-of-your-seat tension junkies who enjoy sorting through facts with an unreliable narrator at the helm. The mystery of who exactly is that mysterious woman who briefly occupied a cruise liner cabin and then suddenly disappeared provides further intrigue in this twist-and-turn plot that keeps readers guessing until the end.

Laura "Lo" Blacklock has a problem. Actually, she's facing quite a few challenges: her apartment in England was burgled while she was at home, sending her into an emotional tailspin. On top of that, she drinks too much, she's on anti-depressants, she's broken up with her boyfriend—though she's not sure about that—and now her dream assignment on a posh luxury yacht as a reporter for a travel magazine is turning into the trip from hell. Lo's penchant for excessive alcohol consumption and her fragile state from the trauma of encountering a thief in her home, immediately sets the stage for readers to rally behind the confused young woman. But her instability also makes it unclear if her account of events that involved a body tossed overboard really happened.

In the spirit of Agatha Christie's closed room whodunits, the list of suspects is limited to the Scandinavian staff and the ship's passengers because the person who committed a possible murder is at sea. The perpetrator could be anyone, fellow journalists, photographers, and wealthy people paying for the privilege of participating in the "The Aurora's" maiden voyage through the Norwegian fjords. But the list seems to narrow as clues point in the direction of Lo's former boyfriend, Ben, a dashing photographer named Cole Lederer who's having problems with his wife, or the ship's head of security, Johann Nilsson. Still, there are enough red herrings to keep readers scratching their heads.

Ruth Ware brilliantly foretells snippets of future events in the story at chapter conclusions using social media in the form of emails and chat rooms of amateur  detectives. She also has a talent for keeping readers wondering if our narrator is a drunken fool or a broken woman prone to hallucinations. It is no surprise that *The Woman in Cabin 10* was an Instant New York Times and USA Today bestseller.

Ruth Ware grew up in Sussex, on the south coast of England. After graduating from Manchester University, she moved to Paris before settling in North London. She is the internationally bestselling author of *In a Dark, Dark Wood* and *The Lying Game* (2017). She is married with two small children. *The Death of Mrs. Westaway* is due to be released at the end of June 2018. Fans of *The Girl on the Train* by Paula Hawkins and *Gone Girl* by Gillian Flynn will probably enjoy this book.

Luckiest Girl Alive

Luckiest Girl Alive by Jessica Knoll (2016, Simon & Schuster, paperback, 368 pages, $9.51) has been compared to Gone Girl by Gillian Flynn and Girl on a Train by Paula Hawkins. This debut mystery novel certainly delivers on the unexpected twists and turns of these two popular novels. The *Luckiest Girl Alive's* story is narrated by Ani (pronounced awnee), short for "Tiffany," and oscillates between current time where twenty-eight-year-old Ani is obsessed with losing weight for her upcoming wedding to wealthy Luke Harrison and fourteen-year-old Tiffany's first year at prestigious Bradley High School.

Adult Ani is thriving at The Woman's Magazine, where she writes a sex advice column and is positioned to write serious pieces for The New Yorker when the two magazines merge. Ani seems to have it all and her cynicism initially makes her seem ungrateful and, therefore, unlikeable. At times she is cold, calculating, manipulating, but at the same time somehow compelling. We soon learn that her love for her fiancée has waned and Ani is questioning her decision to marry Luke.

Meanwhile, as the new kid in the prestigious school, young Tiffany is determined to be accepted by the popular kid crowd. Her ambitions soon cause her to make foolish mistakes, particularly in her teenage love life. Although she's romantically interested in a fellow newcomer to the school named Liam, she settles for Dean, a cruel boy with less than noble intentions. She's also obsessed with her English teacher/track coach, Mr. Larson. Eventually, relegated to outcast status from the "in" kids, Tiffany befriends Arthur who has a big chip on his shoulder. Little does Tiffany know she's about to get in way over her head. As her childhood story and upbringing come to light, her character flaws begin to make sense. Tiffany's narcissistic mother, a social climber more concerned with other's opinions, combined with her emotionally-distant father contribute to Ani's complex personality.

Ani's past and present collide when Ani returns to her childhood town to film a documentary about the events that she endured during her first years of high school. Determined to reunite with her former teacher who is now married with children, Ani manipulates Mr. Larson to meet her for drinks. Their reunion leads them back to Bradley, where Ani tries to charm her mentor into an affair.

Luckiest Girl Alive was a New York Times best seller. It was nominated for the Edgar Award for Best First Novel by an American author and the 2015 Goodreads Choice Award for Best Debut Author. Since its release in 2015, more than 450,000 copies have been sold. The book spent four months on best-seller lists and Reese Witherspoon has optioned the film rights. Jessica Knoll has been a senior editor at Cosmopolitan and the articles editor at SELF. She lives in New York City with her husband.

HUGH'S FRIEND
by Mark Towse

When I speak to my friends we often joke and reminisce about the imaginary friends we used to have as kids, sometimes we would play or discuss things with them and even argue with them, perhaps it was just an instinctive way of preparing ourselves for growing up.

The general rule of thumb is they would come out on request, when you needed them, when you wanted to play or just not be alone. My imaginary friend was called Hugh. He was two years older than me and an exception to the rule, and I thought he was a prick.

Sitting at the dinner table one day, and as my Mum was reaching for the veggies, he slipped under and came back up holding his nose and gagging, he told me my Mum wasn't wearing any knickers. He also said he caught my Dad playing with himself in the shower earlier and he wasn't goddamn surprised. I intentionally dropped my fork to prove he was just telling tales, I promised myself I would invent a time machine to take me back and grip that fork with everything I had. I didn't eat much that afternoon.

Some things he told me were truths; others were just outright lies designed to ruin self-confidence and to push anxiety levels through the roof, and he thought this was hilarious. For example, on my seventh birthday, he told me I was adopted and the papers were in the third drawer down of my Mum's dresser. All I found was a bunch of knickers and bras, and what looked to be a torch that vibrated. Hugh told me that my Mum used to shove the torch so far up her fanny you could see her tonsils. Obviously, I didn't believe him. He lied about the adoption and the torch, and he was full of shit.

At this point he had also told me that my Mum was sleeping with the postman and that my Dad was a serial killer, so you can see what I was dealing with.

When Hugh told me there was someone else living at the house, another child, I dismissed it immediately. Hugh said he could prove it but I'd had enough, to be honest; I actually tried to unimagine him from my mind for a good couple of weeks before I realized the stubborn little prick wasn't going anywhere.

The first day at school, already a hard enough time for a seven-year-old to get his head around, was something I will never forget. The teacher placed me next to some kid called Robert. He seemed nice enough, but Hugh seemed jealous that I had even said hello to the kid.

down the hallway and towards the back end of the house.

"You'll see soon enough," is all he replied as he finally made it to the cellar door.

My Dad always said the cellar was a work in progress and too dangerous for us to go in, I always wondered why it didn't apply to him though.

"Hugh, I am not allowed in there,

see nothing else worth noting.

"Push that last panel, Jack," he said.

I did and it moved inwards, not just a little bit, and I soon realized it was a makeshift door.

"How do you know all this, Hugh?" I asked inquisitively.

'Go inside, Jack,"

As I stepped inside and swept the torch around, I shrieked and dropped it, I scrambled on the floor in a mix of fear and panic and finally felt the handle and pointed it forwards again. The little boy there covered his eyes and I moved the torch to the left out of his direct line of sight. He cowered in the corner and I noticed the chain attached to the bolt in the floor, and a plate and glass on the mattress next to him.

"This is Peter," Hugh replied very casually.

"Why are you in our house, Peter?" I asked very naively.

In my ear all day, "you're a homo, you're a homo," and slightly more inventive "Jack and Bobby sitting in a tree, Jack blows Bobby, one-two-three."

That carried on all day. "You're a homo, you're a homo," until I lost the plot and screamed at the top of my lungs in front of the entire classroom. "I'm not a fucking homo!" Some of the kids laughed, some went white, the teacher did neither but did escort me from the class.

Mum picked me up early that day. She was very disappointed indeed, not that I wasn't a homosexual, but my behavior let her down considerably. Hugh was still unbelievably pleased with himself and asked me to follow him; he had something to show me.

"Where are we going?" I called out to him in pursuit as he sprinted ahead

even Mum isn't."

"Do you ever think to yourself why not?" he asked as he pointed to a jar on top of the cupboard. I grabbed the key from it, pushed it into the hole and turned the handle, the air conditioner was already on and it was pretty cool in that space, I remember. I flicked the light switch on but nothing happened. "Oh yes, in the cupboard next to the door," Hugh said, so I went back and grabbed the torch. I saw the vast array of jars and bottles of wine spread across various tables and felt my way along the walls.

"What are we doing here, Hugh?" I asked impatiently.

"Keep going, nearly there," he replied.

I kept edging along the wall and finally came to the end of the room; I flashed the torch around and could

Peter didn't say anything, he just sat shaking.

"You need to ask your Dad that," Hugh replied.

As I turned around to shine the torch towards Hugh I saw the etchings on the wooden interior of the room.

"Hugh was here."

ABOUT THE AUTHOR:

Mark is 44 years of age, married with two children and lives in Melbourne Australia. He has only just rediscovered his passion for writing and his pen is smoking.

Mark is currently working in sales and marketing but would sell his soul to the devil for a full time career as a writer. Some of his other stories will be published shortly. Follow him twitter.com/marktowsey12

Story Photo credit: Aleksandr Belugin | 123RF.

THE FIRES OF TONY PHILLIPS

Author, Journalist, Commentator

Q: You studied philosophy, written political commentary for the Huffington Post and others, had a weekly column, and written fiction and non-fiction works from novels, short stories and poetry. How did your interest in philosophy become a literary career, and was there one moment that stood out as a catalyst?

A: I think my interest in philosophy is actually second in the hierarchy; my love of the word came first. I was very fortunate to study under an older crop of professors for whom philosophy was still steeped in Classicism, before the discipline got co-opted and pressed into service as meta-theory and step-child to the hard sciences. My immersion in philosophy taught me noting about what to think. It did, however, teach me how to think.

Whether I'm writing some caustic social satire or finding humor in the banal for a weekly editorial, or delving into some comparative analysis or trying my hand at literature for its own sake, I always look for the possible lurking behind the actual. Fiction, to me, is hypothetical reality and thus science fiction, as I approach it, is the-not-yet-real but easily hypothesized truth we can see just around the corner. The details don't emerge in sharp definition, but the shape of things to come is evident in the shadows.

And then there's this – writing is, for lack of a better word, sexy. I don't mean that it will get you a date (though it might). I mean that to myself, when I write, I feel elegant, self-indulged and gratified. It's an evocative practice. It revs up the senses and heightens experience.

So, if there's one moment that stands out to me as a launching point for a writing career, it would be in 1993. I got a gig writing a recurring column for a publishing industry magazine and the first time I saw my own work in print I felt the sensual satisfaction of the work itself amplified a thousand times. I had stopped performing in front of the mirror and taken my performance to the stage. From that moment onward, writing has been a daily part of my life. It's an addiction and I don't want to recover.

Q: Political commentary is a dangerous practice these days, and certainly one aspect of it is the fallout from those of opposing views. Without details, that surely would "offend" half the reading audience, how have those skills helped you bridge into the science fiction realm of "The Fires of Orc," your 2017 novel?

A: Irony deficiency is a scourge on the land. Seriously. Some things are just funny, whether a vast readership recognizes it or not. Likewise, as a people we Westerners are beset by the plague of one-sidedness. People need to get a grip and recognize that not every critique is an attack. There can be more than one fair observation about any given phenomenon, principle, practice or orientation. The world is not black-and-white. Neither should it be red-and-blue. I realize every time I write anything with a political viewpoint I run the real risk of driving away half of all people. And since I don't feel beholden to one ideology or another, by now I should have driven away virtually everyone.

Still, however, folks keep reading.

When I first conceived of the premise for The Fires of Orc, Donald Trump was still just a loudmouth with a former silly television franchise and the bewildering power to bankrupt casinos. It was 2013 and it occurred to me that there are ways to game the perverse American electoral system. The law of big numbers means that usually winners win, but as mathematicians will point out and history has shown, there are plenty of ways for losers to win. If one knows the tricks and one is backed by the power to manipulate opinion through control of the cyberverse, well then anything is possible. I didn't foresee that possibility as a near-term reality. But three years later it came to pass.

In the book I imagined the ability to control popular opinion through the power of quantum computing. It turns out we didn't even need that near-future innovation for the trick to work. I'll say this for Trump; he was way ahead of my own vision for mass manipulation.

Q: What is your writing practice like? Do

you write first, edit later, have set writing times and places?

A: This is one of those questions serious writers are supposed to answer seriously. I should probably talk about what hat I don, cocked at what jaunty angle, and what gin paired with what dark chocolate sits on what corner of my desk beneath what leaded-glass window in what corner of the attic on what winter's day, while I, in fingerless gloves, hunch over my loose-leaf pad, toiling away by oil lamp light until I hear my muse and my heart thrums to her clarion call. All that is insipid romanticism. It's the sort of thing writers talk about to make writing seem like something it's not.

I write haphazardly, extemporaneously and spontaneously. Essay-length work I don't even outline. I formulate key sentences then write around them. For a book-length work, I create chapter headings as a rough structural guideline and I write the text in nearly finished voice. I go back and edit when the whole work is through.

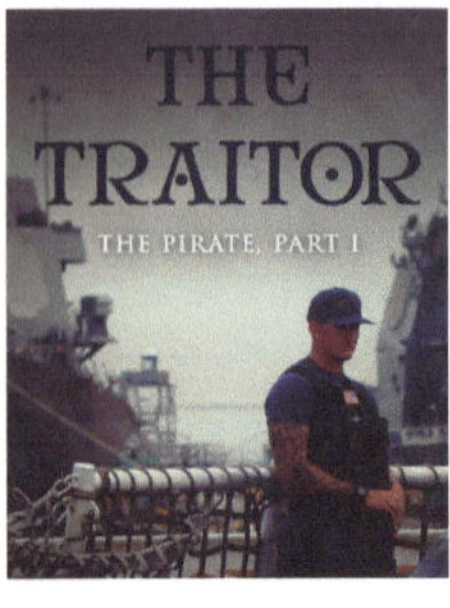

I'm extremely impatient with the writing process. I love the product and I only endure its creation for the joy I take in its finished form. Approaching it the way I do makes it much easier to throw out the stuff that doesn't work. If you write every day, much of what you write is sure to be terrible. I don't invest myself so deeply that I can't bear to toss out the failures. I write whenever I feel like it and however I can. Doing it otherwise would feel forced and formulaic. I'm more interested in what I'm thinking and how I'm feeling in the moment than I am in what the serious author side of myself might churn out under contrived conditions.

Q: Apple or PC? Fountain pen, ball pen or pencil? Notebook (computer) or notepad? Coffee or tea while writing (or a Hemingway concoction?)

A: I own pens but I can never find any. I use paper to take notes in meetings. I compose entirely on my keyboard. Coffee is made round the clock in my house. I used to write with the aid of a good bourbon but I found that what sounds good with a snootfull is usually awful in the sober light of day.

Q: Any advice for writers looking for best practices?

A: I can think of two best practices I encourage all writers to follow. First, and this is axiomatic, write. You might think you write copiously but I promise you, when you're all written out there's someone else still writing. In addition to my own writing, I write as a contractor for two dozen private and public agencies. Most of it is word salad, but I write an average of several thousand words a day, five to six days a week. In the past quarter-century I've written nearly 20 million words. I like a few hundred thousand of them. The point is to just get the words out and let your voice develop its own memory, form its own habits and follow its own course. Think of it as a combat sport. You're not ready to go 12 rounds in the ring until you've done 12,000 in the gym.

Secondly, and this one is pretty familiar but deserves emphasis, forget that English permits superfluous use of the verb 'to be.' There is no reason to say, "It was raining…" when "it rained" will do. Find all the passive verbs and past continuous tenses and had-been-having-had-tos and other barbaric features of our ignominious tongue and rip those from your text like you would a stray whisker from your grandmother's chin. I spend many a waking hour reading governmentese, replete with atrocities like "It has been proven that one is at increased risk of mortality while one is driving if one's attention is distracted by being involved in other activities…" which is much better expressed by the simple phrase, "Texting and driving kills people." Thus, in a nutshell, write all the time and cut the tortured English formations.

> "Irony deficiency is a scourge on the land. Seriously. Some things are just funny, whether a vast readership recognizes it or not. Likewise, as a people we Westerners are beset by the plague of one-sidedness. People need to get a grip and recognize that not every critique is an attack. There can be more than one fair observation about any given phenomenon, principle, practice or orientation." ~Tony Phillips

Alan Brennert: People's Choice & Emmy Award Winner

by Jill Hedgecock

Novels and Screenplays and the Flexibility of Writing Both

Q: In one paragraph, tell us about your new book, Daughter of Moloka'i.

A: It's a sequel—or more accurately, a "companion tale"—to Moloka'i that tells the story of Ruth Utagawa, the daughter that Rachel Kalama was forced to give up at birth. It follows young Ruth from her arrival at the Kapi'olani Home for Girls in Honolulu, to her adoption by a Japanese couple who raise her on a farm in California, to her marriage and unjust internment at Manzanar during World War II—and then, after the war, to the life-altering day when she receives a letter from a woman who says she is Ruth's birth mother, Rachel. Daughter of Moloka'i expands upon Ruth and Rachel's 22-year relationship, only hinted at in Moloka'i, complementing the first book; together they form one large, overarching story.

Q: What do you see as the biggest difference between writing a novel and a screenplay?

A: A screenplay is a blueprint for a film, and my job as a screenwriter is to tell the story through action, dialog, and minimal scene description. But when I'm writing a novel I'm not just the writer, I'm the director, the actors, the location scout, the set dresser, the wardrobe supervisor—I have to create the entire world of the story in words. Each medium has its own challenges and its own rewards. Mostly I enjoy having the control of a story that a novel affords, but I admit there are times when I'm describing what someone is wearing or what a room look like that I ask rhetorically, "Isn't there a department head who can do this for me?"

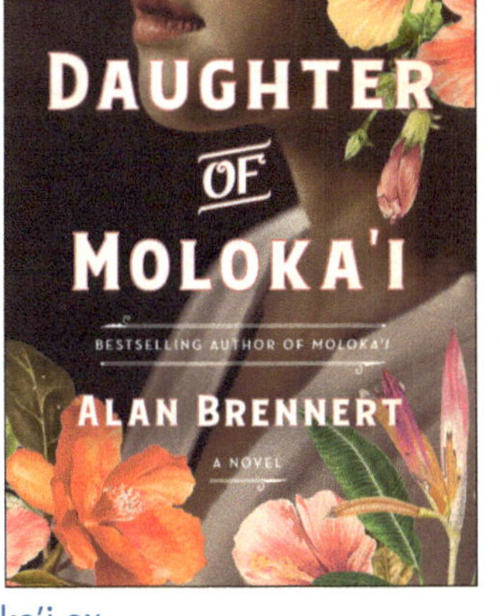

Q: Tell us about winning an Emmy for your work on the television show, L.A. Law, in 1991. Did you get more satisfaction for this achievement, for the People's Choice Award, or for winning the Nebula Award for "Ma Qui"?

A: The Emmy was something I had dreamed about winning since I was a kid—literally. Growing up, my idols were writers like Rod Serling, Paddy Chayefsky, Ernest Kinoy, James Costigan—the men behind the "golden age of television" of the 1950s (most of which I didn't experience firsthand, being a bit too young, but discovered through reruns and movies). So it was quite a rush being up on stage at the Pasadena Civic Auditorium when L.A. Law won for Best Drama Series. But I'm very proud of my Nebula Award as well, since that was a validation of, and my first award for, my literary work.

Q: What authors or people have most influenced your writing career?

A: It's an eclectic mix: authors like F. Scott Fitzgerald, Nathanael West, Jonathan Strong and Ray Bradbury; playwrights like Robert Anderson and Thornton Wilder; and the aforementioned Serling, Costigan, et al. I've gone on to write in all those media—books, a play, film—and I like to think I continue to be influenced by good work in each field. (Moloka'i, as I've said elsewhere, was inspired by a fine novel called Consider This, Señora by Harriet Doerr, Honolulu shows influences of the work of Arthur Golden and Lisa See, and Palisades Park owes something to Larry McMurtry's The Desert Rose).

Q: I understand that you transformed one of your first novels, Time and Chance, into a screenplay. When you revisited this work, where did you see your biggest improvement as a writer over time? Was reworking this novel like visiting an old friend?

A: I had the opportunity to bring Time and Chance back into print a few years ago, and in the process I found myself doing a fairly heavy polish on it. I didn't change anything in the story, just polished or simplified the prose where it seemed too flowery or where the syntax was a bit rococo. I performed what I like to call a "semi-colonectomy," deleting vast numbers of unnecessary commas, semi-colons, dashes, and ellipses that I would not use when writing a novel today. It made me realize that my prose style has evolved since 1990 (when Time and Chance was published)—it's cleaner, leaner, smoother.

Q: What was your favorite novel or screenplay to write?

A: The novel I enjoyed most was Moloka'i. I got up every day excited to begin work, because I was writing about a place that I loved—Hawai'i—and a little-known part of history that no one else had approached in quite this way. I did my research in the morning, wrote in the afternoon until dinnertime, and often went back to my computer in the evening if I

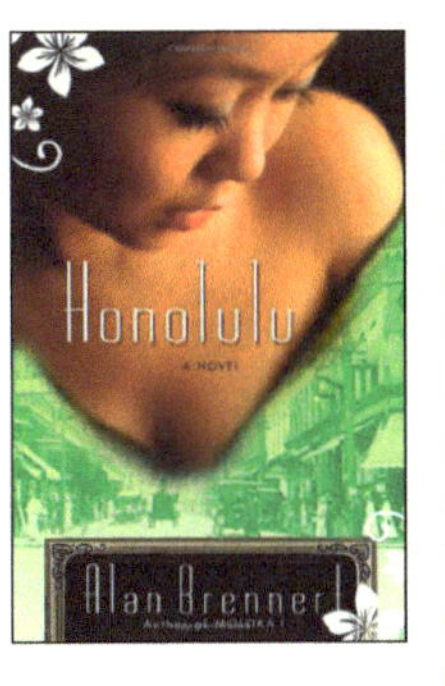

had a problem that still had to be resolved or if a new idea had occurred to me that I wanted to get down. I felt something similar writing Daughter of Moloka'i: after spending decades in television and film writing mainly other people's characters, here I was writing a follow-up about my own characters, and expanding their personal backgrounds in the kind of depth and detail I've rarely been allowed to explore in film. That was exhilarating.

Q: Do you enjoy book tours or writing more?

A: I'm essentially an introvert who can be extroverted when the occasion demands (you have to be to work in Hollywood, where you collaborate daily with so many people). So although I do enjoy book tours and meeting readers, I'm at heart happiest when sitting in a room writing. Or in Hawai'i, doing research!

I hope you've enjoyed hearing about Alan Brennert. To learn more, visit his website http://www.alanbrennert.com.

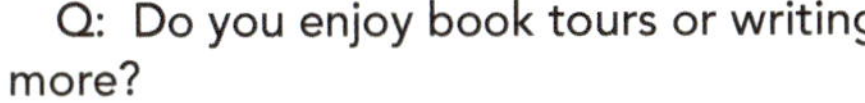

STUART HORWITZ
AUTHOR OF FINISH YOUR BOOK IN THREE DRAFTS

by Jill Hedgecock
www.jillhedgecock.com

Is 2018 the year that you're going to finally find time to tackle that bucket list goal of writing a book? Stuart Horwitz has devised a technique to help you fulfill that dream. Regardless of whether your writing fiction, a memoir or nonfiction, Finish Your Book in Three Drafts provides the tools you need using straightforward guidance with a splash of humor.

In this interview, learn about Horowitz and the insights he's gained as the founder and principal of Book Architecture, a firm of independent editors based in Providence and Boston.

Q: In one paragraph, can you give us some highlights from Finish Your Book in Three Drafts?

A: It's not just marketing, I swear! You can Finish Your Book in Three Drafts whether you're writing fiction or nonfiction, whether you're an outliner who meticulously scripts every writing session or a pantser who pilots solely by feel. Because you don't want to be writing the same book for the rest of your life.

Three drafts. That's all you need.

• The messy draft: which is all about getting it down.

• The method draft: which is all about making sense.

• The polished draft: which is all about making it good.

You can Finish Your Book in Three Drafts provided you approach each draft in the right spirit, and know what action steps to take between drafts.

Q: Describe your most memorable moment as an author.

A: I've now completed over 80 tour dates throughout North America in the past four-plus years. But no matter how exciting life post-publication has been, it has never gotten better than those champion writing sessions where I was achieving the height of my flight. When someone says, "Your books are so original; I

have learned more from you than anyone else" — I am happy, of course — but it is like I am hearing about a trip they've taken when I got left home.

Nothing will ever beat those rare nights when I knew I nailed it. When I had prepared for a writing session, and executed, while welcoming the unexpected. And then went to go smoke a cigar in the heart of Providence. I might have been thinking about the people who inspired me, but sitting there it was just me, myself, and I.

So my point is that we need to take writing and separate it from publishing. What writing has done for me exists outside of what has been published, and far exceeds it in value.

Q: What authors have most influenced your writing?

A: This is a hard question to answer. I mean, it probably numbers in the hundreds, right? I will just say when I saw a bibliography and my name appeared between Hesse, Hermann and Kafka, Franz, I thought. I am ready to die now in peace. Except for the kids I still have to raise and not wanting to leave a widow, that kind of thing.

Q: What are the biggest mistakes you see in author's manuscripts?

A: This is a big question! I'd say the following five are the biggest structural mistakes I

see — as I spend a lot of my time thinking about structure:

1. What you're writing isn't what you think you're writing.

Not that it's that far off, necessarily. Let's say you've set sail—to use an extended marine metaphor—heading for an island. Everyone needs some "sea room," and now you've landed on some neighboring coast. Writing is a largely unconscious activity. At some point, we need to become conscious enough to see how we might get the reader and ourselves safely home. Some writers don't want to be made conscious at any point during their process. In my experience, more often than not, they drift.

2. You have not generated enough material to begin revising.

One of my clients was delighted with her first assignment, which was to generate fifty pages of crap. Her next assignment was to generate another fifty, making a hundred pages of crap. There is no substitute for not having generated enough material before you begin revising.

3. You want to put too much stuff in.

A chef whose cookbook I worked on called it the "kitchen-sink" syndrome: a beginner makes a marinara sauce by using every vegetable in the refrigerator, and every spice on the rack. They use seventeen ingredients when there really should just be tomatoes, garlic, and like four other things. You want to be able to taste the Parmesan shavings.

Writers think, How am I supposed to fill up a whole book's worth of pages unless I include everything I can think of? Unity, the sense that your book is only about one thing—that the reader can trust you know how to drive this thing—cannot be achieved by trying to make things comprehensive.

4. You let too many people read it before it was ready.

Why is this a structural problem? Because when you involve beta readers (people who read your draft when you know it isn't done), you are far more open to feedback than you will be at a later stage. You may lose time and focus by pursuing a direction that someone else recommended rather than discovering the path which you really want to travel.

5. Your narrator is too much like you.

In fact, basically, it is you. This is not as much a problem in certain non-fiction genres (like a blog), when it is considered great to sound as much like yourself as possible. Sounding like yourself while opening out to universal experience, is called "finding your voice."

In fiction, however, you need maximum flexibility to explore emotions and imagine events that will embody those emotions. If your narrator is bound by only who you think you are, as opposed to who you might become, your writing can go stale.

Q: Who is your idol?

A: My idol is my cat. He recently got in a fight with a fishercat — vicious animals that live in the Northeast that are like wolverines, and he had to have an eye removed.

While the procedure was going on, he was licking the doctor's hand, giving him love because he knew the man was trying to help him.

Me? I come from a family where when we have a fever of 99 degrees we're "in bed with a little something." So I want to be more like my cat.

P.S. He has been getting along tremendously well without an eye and his hunting skills have not diminished in the least. Except every now and then he bangs into a chair and then makes off across the room like nothing happened.

I hope you've enjoyed learning about Stuart Horwitz.

To learn more visit his website: http://bookarchitecture.com where you can sign up for his newsletter.

All About ~~Aditing~~ Editing

by Jeri Walker
JeriWB.com

All manuscripts need multiple rounds of editing. Polishing a book's language makes little sense if content issues haven't been ironed out and vice versa. An author's publishing goals can also dictate where funds are best spent, and good beta readers and critique partners can certainly prove valuable.

The major types of editing include content editing, stylistic editing, and copy-editing. While some blurring of lines inevitably occurs, each type of editing serves a distinct purpose. It doesn't help matters either that editing terms are often used interchangeably. This is why requesting an editing sample and signing a contract for services is so important.

Content editing deals with organization and deeper meaning, and it also goes by the most names. Developmental editing is big picture editing that often falls under the umbrella of book coaching. On the other hand, a substantive edit (also called structural or comprehensive editing) is a heavy edit that typically combines multiple levels of editing on a completed manuscript.

Manuscript evaluations are also called editorial reports, reader reports, critiques, or assessments and can be stand-alone documents or done in conjunction with comments made directly in the margins. This type of content editing focuses on developmental feedback concerning story elements, marketability, as well as any glaring language use issues.

Stylistic editing, which is often called line editing, deals more with shaping language and making it a pleasure to read. On the other hand, copy-editing focuses on correcting errors to ensure consistency, cohesiveness, and completeness. The last step in the process is proofreading, which should ideally take place after a manuscript has been formatted for publication. Often, Indie authors think only a proofread is sufficient before publishing, but it most certainly is not!

When choosing an editor, word of mouth is a great place to start. Beyond that, take the time to explore a potential editor's portfolio as well as to read client testimonials. Editors with big publishing house credit will cost top-dollar, but many mid-price editors will work just as well and likely have more openings. If your budget is minuscule, you might luck out and find and up-and-coming editor who doesn't charge much. However, is that a risk worth taking? Buyer beware.

Also consider the editor's overall background given how there is no standard editing certificate available in the US. A serious editor should also maintain at least one affiliation with a professional editing organization. Take the time to assess how much experience the editor has in your genre, especially when seeking developmental editing.

So what does an editor charge? That depends on many factors, but keep in mind a freelancer who charges $50 an hour is likely only really making $25 after taxes, expenses, savings, etc. Pricing may be project-based, per word, or per hour. Extensive research has revealed the following ranges:

- Developmental Editing $3,710-$5,512
- Manuscript Evaluation $770-$2,880
- Line Editing $2,800-$4,000
- Copyediting $1,088-$2,176
- Proofreading $750-$1,050

Gulp. Never fear. There are worse things you could spend money on, right?

AUG 2018
BOOKS 'N PIECES
A Magazine for Writers and Readers

MADE IN
IDAHO
MADE IN

IDAHO'S
BESTSELLING
AUTHOR

JOANNE
PENCE

SHORT STORIES:
CHARLES HITCHCOCK: THE LAST LAUGH JIM HASSE: NOTHING
TO FEAR PAT TOMKINS: AMONG THE BRIARS MARK TOWSE:
HUGH'S FRIEND

INTERVIEWS:
OANNE PENCE (COVER) TONY PHILLIPS ALAN BRENNERT
STUART HORWITZ PETER JAMES: INTERNATIONAL BESTSELLING
CRIME AUTHOR MARC RAINER ELLIS KNOX LAURA C. LEFKOWITZ
WRITERS ON THE EDGE

ARTICLES:
JERI WALKER WINE WHILE WRITING ALL ABOUT EDITING JILL
HEDGECOCK BOOK REVIEWS WRITER GUIDELINES

MISCELLANEOUS:
BIG WORDS FACEBOOK WRITING GROUPS BOOKSTORE 'N PIECES
BOOK FREEBIES

Cover photo: Sherry Briscoe Photography.

www.BooksNPieces.com

Joanne Pence: Award-Winning, Bestselling Author and Co-Founder of The Idaho Writer's Guild

Joanne Pence is an award-winning, USA Today best-selling author of the Angie Amalfi and Rebecca Mayfield mysteries, historical fiction, contemporary romance, romantic suspense, fantasy and supernatural novels.

Making her home in the Boise foothills, she was one of the founders, and current board member, of the Idaho Writer's Guild, a strong supporter of local authors, and a very approachable person.

She has also been president of the Boise chapter of Sisters in Crime, board member of the Popular Fiction Association of Idaho, and has held offices in the California Writers Club. A graduate of U.C. Berkeley with a master's degree in journalism, Joanne has written for magazines, worked for the federal government, and taught school in Japan.

Q: You are a founder of the Idaho Writers' Guild, now only one of two such groups in Idaho. Why did you decide that Idaho needed this group, and has it met your expectations?

A: When I first moved to Boise, I learned of several local organizations for writers of specific fiction genres, such as mystery, romance, and fantasy. As I spoke with those writers, we realized that we shared many issues, regardless of genre. Several of us—who became founders of the Idaho Writers Guild (IWG)—believed it would be helpful to have one group for authors to join no matter what they were writing, non-fiction as well as fiction, genre fiction as well as literary. We also recognized that many of the already established groups emphasized "how to's" for beginning writers—how to plot, how to develop characters, how to handle point of view, etc. We wanted to create a guild that would also benefit established writers in areas such as

marketing, publicity, burn-out, and networking.

IWG has grown beyond my expectations, and I hope it will continue to thrive. I am constantly amazed by the number of well-established, well-known authors in our community. IWG is a great venue to for the authors to meet for informal, useful discussions and sharing.

Q: You were born and raised in the San Francisco Bay Area, but the Boise foothills has been your home for quite some time. What made you settle in Boise?

A: Would you believe I discovered this area because of my writing? Back in the late 1990s, I was invited to Boise to give a talk at a combined Coeur du Bois (romance) and Partners in Crime (mystery) conference. I enjoyed it so much, that when I was invited back to present another workshop, I asked my husband to join me. We both loved the foothills, the people, the way of life—even the weather. We took a couple of vacations here, and when my husband retired, we decided to make Boise our home. We've never had a moment's regret.

Q: You've won many awards for your novels, and enjoy a notable success.

How long did it take you to reach that point in your writing when you knew that you had "made it" as a professional author?

A: I wish I could say "overnight." But as with most authors, it has taken many years. My first book was published in 1988 (when I was ten years old—I wish). My second wasn't published until 1993. After that, I wrote one mystery each year for a number of years, published by HarperCollins. Everything

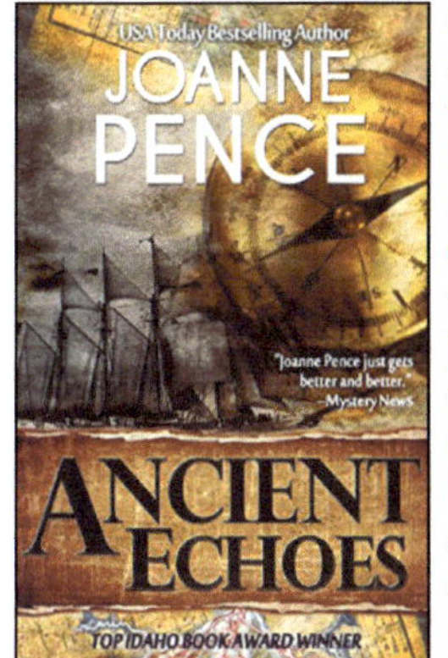

changed in 2012 when I wrote a "supernatural suspense" thriller that took place in Idaho. I quickly realized that New York publishers didn't really know what to do with such a book. At the time, "Indie" publishing was just beginning, so I decided to give it a try. The book, Ancient Echoes, did surprisingly well, so I branched out to other books, and started a second mystery series. To my amazement, publishing my own books and establishing my own publishing company has been more rewarding to me in every sense of the word than being with a big New York publisher. It was, however, a very long and winding road.

Q: Any advice to new writers, especially Idaho writers, looking to make a career in writing?

A: If you want to be a writer, you have

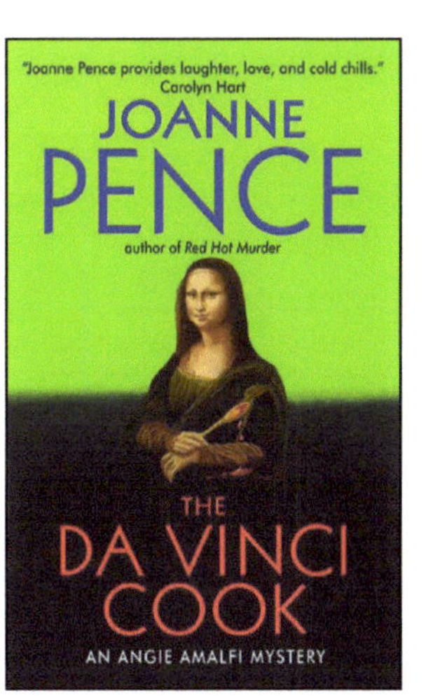

to enjoy the actual writing process because that's what you'll spend most of your time doing. In many of my workshops, I meet people who want to "have written"—but they don't want to devote the hours and hours required to write something that other people want to read. Also, remember that writing is a craft. Some inspiration is needed, but 99% of it is simply writing, rewriting, and working to perfect the craft to become as good at it as you can. Last, find ways to meet other writers through groups such as IWG, and don't hesitate to talk about problems, stumbling blocks, and so on, troubling you. Other writers understand what you're going through better than anyone else. We might even have words of encouragement and advice. And, more than anything else, keep writing.

I love hearing from writers and readers. You can contact me at joanne@joannepence.com.

Visit Joanne's author page at Amazon: https://amzn.to/2uWduDh

Website: http://www.joannepence.com/

Twitter:@JoannePence

Ellis Knox

LIVING THE ALTEARTH WRITER LIFE

Ellis Knox has been a medieval historian, a computer support tech, and a university webmaster, but he has retired from all that to write books. He was a pioneer in Online education, offering the first college credit history course that was fully web-based (in 1994). He has published scholarly articles but now writes only fantasy fiction. His publications include the novels *Goblins at the Gates*, and *A Child of Great Promise*, two novelettes (*Mad House* and *The Garden of Hugo Vuerloz*) and two short stories (*The Roadmaster* and *The Carrotfinger Man*). All are Altearth tales.

Q: You've been a lifelong writer, immersed in medieval and early European history, complete with degrees and a career as a college professor on these subjects. With all that background, what took you so long to decide on a writing career, and what was your catalyst that cemented that idea?

A: That word "decide" is the key. I have indeed been writing all my life. I was forever doing world building of one sort or another, and writing stories that I never finished, save for one. I wrote a short story around 1973 and sent it off to SF magazines. I got a rejection letter from H.L. Gold, a hand-written note that said no thanks but keep trying. Or words to that effect. But I was getting seriously involved in becoming a historian at that point and I did not try again.

Then, about thirty years later (!), my wife found that note. She put it on my desk and there was the ghost of Galaxy Magazine telling me to keep trying. For some reason, it clicked. By that time, retirement was within reach, so my decision was not so much to choose writing as a career but simply to get stories told. I was determined not to stand at the end of my life and say I wished I'd written a book.

Q: Why write about the medieval-esque topic, magic, Romans, and so on? What enthralls you about this subject?

A: It stems from the core idea, which I had some time in the mid-1990s. I would take all the myths and legends and monsters of European history, which of course meant magic had to be real. But I would keep as much historical reality as I could. What enthralled me was the prospect of treating two thousand years of history as a kind of musical theme, then riffing on that theme. With so much raw material, I figured I could spend the rest of my life writing stories in that setting.

Q: You've also had extensive computer and Website experience. And, in addition, you're a musician (guitar and piano), and a big gaming enthusiast. How have all these elements helped you in your writing career?

A: Nothing directly. My training as a historian helped immensely. Specifically, I learned how to be critiqued in a professional manner, I learned languages (including proper English), I learned how to research effectively, and how to write long works (my dissertation was about 450 pages long). I do find that I turn to musical analogies when discussing writing. The gaming is almost a hindrance, as I'm keenly aware of how games have worked the same tropes I'm working, and that my readers may well have their ideas about orcs or trolls formed by playing Warcraft, of whatever. The computer background has made me comfortable at my computer, but most of my real tech knowledge is a decade out of date and aging fast.

Q: Your focus is on Altearth? Could you explain what that is and why you chose that focus?

A: I've already mentioned the core idea: monsters and magic are real, the Roman Empire never fell, and I keep all the rest I possible can. Once I came up with the name, Altearth, I knew I had to write at least something in that world. Never waste a good title.

I see no reason to write in any other setting. For one thing, much of the world-building work is already done. I don't have to invent plants and animals, I can just look at photos. I have two thousand years and an entire continent to work with, so there's no end to the stories I can tell. I'm familiar with the history on the Continent, so my stories break out of the usual mold of setting stories in the British Isles or clones thereof. Some people complain that there are too many stories set in medieval Europe, but in truth most are set in the British Isles. Very few are set in Croatia or Navarre or Frisia. And there are whole layers of folklore that almost never appear in modern fantasy. I'm loving it.

Q: How do you write (process)? What parts do you absolutely hate?

A: Six completed stories under my belt and I'm still not sure I have a good answer for that. In my latest, I did quite a bit of planning. In two others I did very little ahead of actual writing.

For the most part, I draft on paper. I love the feel of pen and ink. I like the flexibility--I can sit, lie on the floor, even pace about, whereas the keyboard pretty much nails me to one position. Perhaps most importantly, I can doodle. You can't doodle in a word processor, and I seem to need those few moments in between thoughts. At the keyboard, I tend to hop over to email or do some other distraction. Just for a moment. Hah. But with the pen, I just doodle until my brain picks up again.

I use Scrivener for writing; it's works especially well for breaking the narrative into scenes. I take what I have written by pen, then type that up, usually the same day. That becomes my first editing pass, as I make small adjustments as I move from paper to computer. Once it's in Scrivener, it's all computer-based work from there, though once in a while I'll print out a chapter, especially to make heavy editing notes.

Continues on page 24

MARC RAINER

Stranger Than Fiction: The True Story of a Local Bestselling Author

Charles (Chuck) Ambrose, Jr., is a graduate of the United States Air Force Academy, a former Air Force JAG Circuit Prosecutor and former federal prosecutor with over 30 years experience, who now writes crime dramas under the pen name Marc Rainer. The first book in his five book series hit number-one on Amazon's Kindle store sales rankings for mystery series novels in December 2017.

While he's self-published, he's had over 50,000 sales to date. In addition to his writing, Chuck will be co-chairing the Idaho Writer's Guild's new Mystery Writer's Academy this fall.

Q: You've had over 30 years of experience working in prosecution with the Air Force (JAG), and the Department of Justice. You've also co-authored a manual on how to try murder cases, published by the American Bar Association. At what point in this illustrious career, did you decide that writing crime drama/mystery novels would be the direction for you, and what prompted that?

A: As the saying goes, truth can be stranger than fiction. In my case, it's been a process of merging the two. I came home at night with a lot of natural plot lines from exposure and participation in actual investigations and prosecutions. I'd mention them to my wife, Lea, and her reactions were usually, "You can't make this stuff up," and "You ought to write a book."

As far as what prompted me to write the first book, that's also a combination of things. First, there was Lea's encouragement.

Second, I went to law school with a guy named (John) Grisham who seems to have had some minor success as a writer, and that kind of made me want to try my hand at it. Finally—and perhaps the real driver—was my constantly-triggered gag reflex as I read or watched books, movies, or television shows about the law or police work. We could all recite the usual tropes in our sleep. The tortured soul, lone wolf detective takes on the world's biggest crime organization all by his lonesome and wins, all the while dodging and outrunning machinegun fire, and snap-shooting bad guys off rooftops half a mile away with his handgun.

I wanted to see if I could write compelling crime dramas that were realistic, using real methods, and real legal rules. I use a lot of actual events, techniques, and even trial transcripts in my novels, changing the names to protect both the innocent and the guilty.

Q: What's your writing process like? Computer/notepad, set writing time?

A: Being retired from my day job, I want to enjoy writing, so I write when I get the urge, using either my desktop or a laptop. The laptop goes with us on trips, in case inspiration strikes on the road. I sometimes find myself busier in retirement than when I was "working," but I have the flexibility now to write when it feels like I should.

I don't have any set routine with the books. They percolate when they're ready to do so, and I don't force them. While I've never had "writer's block," I do wait on writer's motivation. To steal a line from an old winery commercial, I will sell no crime before its time.

Q: Why did you decide to self-publish as opposed to going the mainstream publishing route? Any regrets?

A: I was actually one of the 5% who was "lucky" enough

to land an agent with my first manuscript. Unfortunately, I wasn't lucky enough to land a good one. She was lazy, and aside from firing out a few emails, she basically did nothing but keep me out of print for the year of the contract.

With that bad taste in my mouth for the "traditional" process, I happened to read that Amazon had bought Create Space, and decided to try the self-publishing game. The first couple of months were anything but encouraging, but

by the fourth month, "Capital Kill," my first novel, was selling more than 1,000 copies per month.

The success of that book was encouraging enough for me to write the other books in the series, which have sold a total of more than 50,000 copies to date (including the e-book sales).

I have no regrets about the self-publishing decision. I attended a thriller writers' conference last year, and didn't "pitch" any of the agents who were there. I just went to see what I could learn from the various seminars.

I did have one conversation with an agent, however. She asked me why I wasn't presenting anything to an agent, and I told her how many books I'd sold. I was aware from studying the proves that the average "traditionally published" author makes about seventeen cents off the sale of a paperback in a bookstore, that their books usually go out of print after a first publishing run, and that they are in constant struggles with their editors, agents and publishers. They make an average of about $7,000 per year for all of that agony. I've made that in a very good month. I make 70% off the sale of each e-book, and about two-dollars from each paperback sold. The e-books outsell the paperbacks by 300 to one.

I asked this agent why—instead of using the nineteenth century methodology of soliciting partial manuscripts, getting "pitched," and reading query letters—the members of her publishing firms weren't browsing Amazon, looking for successful Indie authors to recruit and publish. It could be a proven minor league system for the New York houses if they were smart enough to use it that way. They could read finished works, look at the author's sales history, check the reader reviews, and make a much more educated decision on what could sell. Her response was, "There's a lot of crap out there." There is, of course, but much of it is also traditionally published.

The arrogance of the traditional industry remains an obstacle to Indie writers. It's almost impossible to crack one of the best-seller lists, and magazine or newspaper reviews are equally hard to come by for "Indies." I really believe that the traditional publishing industry is now in protection mode, and while it's not yet on life support, the traditional methodology is definitely ailing. Amazon's e-book and hard copy print-on-demand schemes have revolutionized the publishing world, and even "successful" authors have turned to self-publishing rather than the play the old game any longer.

I heard this same agent speaking to another agent following my own presentation on a self-publishing seminar at the conference. One asked the other, "Has he pitched anyone, yet?" The response was, "Why does he need an agent with his sales?" I found that to be very revealing. Every author dreams of that magic, six-figure advance check, but the "A-list" hasn't called me yet. Until it does, no regrets.

Q: You are an Idaho resident. How has the Idaho lifestyle affected what you write, or are they two distinctly separate things?

A: We're still new to Idaho—got here in late 2015—but it has felt like home from the first day we arrived. I spent a few years in the Washington, D.C., United States Attorney's Office, and twenty-five in the Kansas City office. I don't miss the traffic in either place, or the east-coast arrogance in D.C. I went to the Air Force Academy in the early seventies, and have been trying to get back to the mountain west ever since. We're happy to be here. As much as a lifestyle, I find Idaho to be a state of mind that I've always had, so in that sense, you'll certainly find it in my books.

Q: Your book(s) have hit the bestselling rank in the Amazon Kindle Store, and the first in your Jeff Trask Crime Drama series hit number one last December. How do you get your readers and how did you get your book noticed and read, to reach the number one spot?

A: "Capital Kill," the first book in the series, reached the number one sales ranking in the Kindle Store's mystery series category in December. I was humbled and dumbfounded to earn that little banner (No.1 bestseller), even if it only lasted a few hours.

I've found that as an Indie author, there is no magic bullet in terms of publicity. I've tried everything I could think of: radio interviews, blog interviews, sales, giveaways, Facebook ads, mailer ads, movie theater ads, you name it. Nothing hurts, but in the end it comes down to the book, favorable reader reviews, and word-of-mouth recommendations. Marketing is always the challenge, especially for indie authors who don't have a big publishing house behind them. Some authors swear by email and subscriber lists. I don't do those. I find them to be a lot of trouble with a very minimal marginal return on the time and money invested. I don't blog, either. What works for some may not work for others.

Q: You're quite a number of books into this career now. What have you learned about this journey that was a surprise to you when you started?

A: I've had good and bad surprises across the spectrum. On the positive side, I've received a lot of very positive feedback from law enforcement and prosecution professionals who've said, "Finally, someone got it right." On the negative side, the number of hypercritical trolls

who file reviews is astounding, and even more astounding is Amazon's refusal to filter them. I've had one-star reviews listed in which the "reader" admitted that he had not even tried to read the book! I've had folks file reviews who were obviously looking for literary fiction instead of crime thrillers. Every art form is subjective, and you can't even try to please everyone. Overall, the books are being rated at 4.5 stars or higher, so I don't complain about it.

Q: You'll be co-chairing the Idaho Writer's Guild's Mystery Writers' Academy this fall. What attracted you to this and what are your hopes for the academy?

A: Having lived mysteries, investigations, and prosecutions for three decades, I wanted to help lend some experience to writers in the genre. Our hopes for the MWA are mainly to put resources in reach for the authors. We'll have speakers in a lot of the forensic and legal fields. Our hope is that the presentations will be informative, and that our authors can contact our speakers individually in the future if they have more specific questions. Nothing kills a book for me faster than a lack of credibility—like a misstatement of forensic science or legal procedure—and we'll be trying to help our writers avoid those pitfalls.

Q: Idaho is the fastest growing state in the country. We already have a huge writing community, as well as most aspects of the arts. How are you finding all the changes happening, and do you have any concerns for the future?

A: With apologies to our refugees from the coasts, there are very apparent reasons why they left. We don't want to be in California or New York, and we don't want Idaho to become either one. Aside from the politics, those places are anthills of people, with all the problems that one finds in any megalopolis (including the crime rates that I tried to fight my entire career). The Treasure Valley is the right size, the right climate, and has the right kind of people for us. Progress is one thing, but not every change is progress. Living in Meridian, we hope for some solutions to the growing population and traffic issues that don't fundamentally alter the lifestyle here.

A sincere thanks to you and all the others in the field who do NOT have a bias against independent authors. These opportunities are very much appreciated, and they contribute a lot to any success that we're fortunate enough to achieve.

A fact you may not know: The pen name Marc Rainer is Chuck's tribute to two family members whom he lost to cancer: his little brother Marc, and his mother, Betty Rainer Ambrose.

Visit his Website: www.marcrainer.com
Visit his Amazon Author Page: https://amzn.to/2LUFihU

The finished work goes over to Word, off to my editor, rinse and repeat. From Word, it's off to the self-publishing process.

I don't really hate any of it, not even the marketing. Except that I hate all of it at one time or another. Getting all the way to done takes so long, none of it stays fun for the duration. I like to quote Dorothy Parker on this. She said, "I hate writing, but I love having written."

Q: If you could go back to your twenties, is there anything you would do differently in order to achieve your goals faster?

A: Nope. I've thought about this often. I'm sixty-six years old and I have more stories left than I have time left. I'm keenly, achingly aware of that. Even so, I remember me in my twenties. And my thirties. I lacked the discipline. I had to work my way through graduate school to learn how to stay with something to the end. Then I was raising my family and learning a new career, and these things pretty much consumed me.

For better or worse, I had to wait until I was an old man before learning how to undertake the young man's game.

Q: Any marketing/writing advice you can offer our readers?

A: Certainly not in marketing. I haven't sold enough to say anything about what works or doesn't work. But I can say something about writing. I've hinted at it above.

Learn how to finish. This was crucial for me; perhaps I will be for you as well. By "finish" I mean all the way to done. Not just get to THE END, but getting it edited and making the changes. Getting the cover made. Walking yourself through the publishing process. Doing some sort of marketing.

Then finish the second one. Then a third. After the third one, you can look around, take stock. Only by then will you have enough information--not only about the process (from planning through marketing) but also about yourself.

A second piece of advice is, be part of communities. Join writing groups. There's no such thing as the self-taught writer. Be around people. Listen. Learn.

Ellis married his childhood sweetheart in 1969. Together they raised three children. They love to travel and have been to Turkey, Italy, Switzerland, Germany, Russia, Estonia, Sweden, Norway, Denmark, England, and Scotland. "They like to think they are just getting started," he says.

Visit Ellis' Website: https://www.altearth.net/
Ellis' Amazon Author page: https://amzn.to/2AgTNv1

Idaho Writer's Guild Luncheons & Garden City Libations

The Idaho Writers Guild offers a variety of networking and educational opportunities for writers of all genres. Membership is not required to attend some offerings, but opting to pay the modest $50 yearly membership fee results in discounts on workshops, events, and contests as well as a subscription to the monthly newsletter that will keep you in the loop on their offerings.

A main draw for many is the monthly literary luncheons held every third Tuesday (except November and December) at Boise's Riverside Hotel. A variety of guest speakers ensures something for everyone. Plus, it's always nice to commiserate with fellow writers before and after the main talk, because let's face it, writers tend to be a solitary lot. At this time, the talks are not available via webinar.

Another huge draw tied into the Idaho Writers Guild is the yearly two-day writing conference also held at the Riverside Hotel. It's a great chance to chat with literary agents and editors and to hear speakers give advice on the publishing industry. In addition, a handful of fee-based workshops are offered throughout the year, and the free one-hour Writers' Corner workshops happen twice a month at various libraries throughout the Treasure Valley.

A critique group is also available to members. Learning how to give feedback is as equally important as receiving feedback. The Idaho Writers Guild also offers a monthly book club, and it goes without saying that reading widely is a fundamental key in becoming a good writer. Finally, the monthly Saturday Write Track lunches also bring in guest speakers.

With so many offerings, there has never a better time to get involved in Idaho's writing community. More details can be found at idahowritersguild.com.

If you happen to attend the next literary luncheon, why not get some day drinking done in the process? The pairing of writing endeavors and booze is a time-honored tradition. Chinden Boulevard in Garden City is home to numerous breweries, a handful of wineries, and a cidery as well. Not all will be open on a Tuesday afternoon, but there are still plenty of libations to go around.

This relatively short stretch of road has a lot worth exploring, so why not do so with your writer friends in tow? Then again, sipping away an afternoon with your idea notebook in hand isn't a bad idea either. Writers can never go wrong in seeking out experiences in order to gain writing inspiration. To that end, a free shuttle bus runs between Chinden's libation stations in early December in honor of Repeal Day. It's an adventure that will pass in a blur.

Jeri Walker provides manuscript critiques and copyedits for authors who value the intersection of the literary and the commercial. She also forges nonfiction ghostwriting partnerships where her expertise results in prose reflective of the client's voice, experience, and authority. Authenticity is her core guiding value. You can connect with her via Word Bank Writing & Editing at JeriWB.com.

Photo credit: brgfx | 123rf.com

FACEBOOK WRITER GROUPS

if you have to be on Facebook!

Making use of Facebook justifies having an account. Beyond the squabbles, writers can find some great outlets, advice, friends and more. here are just a few that you should checkout:

• Calls for Submission: 54K members of this group must know something! https://www.facebook.com/groups/35517751475/

• Writers Helping Writers is a large group with 75K members. that's a lot of support. https://www.facebook.com/groups/27659251025/

• The Write Life Group offers a supportive environment for all writers. https://www.facebook.com/groups/TheWriteLifeGroup/

• Women Writers, Women's Books: boasts a 15K membership. https://www.facebook.com/groups/WWWB-Magazine/

• Fiction Writers Global is a group that encompasses writers from around the world, a good source of foreign information for your book, perhaps? https://www.facebook.com/groups/fictionwritersgroup/

• 10-Minute Novelists boasts almost 12K members and allows you to break your efforts into smaller sized bits. https://www.facebook.com/groups/488365771285615/

• The Indie Author Group has over 12K members, one of the larger forums that could be of use to you in your writing. https://www.facebook.com/groups/smashwordsauthor/

• Nano Land is a large group of 12K plus people who have particpated in a NanoWrimo. If you have to ask what that is you should really look. https://www.facebook.com/groups/NaNoWriMoparticipants/

Feel free to send us you favorite Facebook writing groups. This will be a permanent feature on our Website at www.BooksNPieces.com

Laura C. Lefkowitz, DVM
Tell-All Tales of An Emergency Veterinarian

Q: How did you develop the idea of an at-home euthanasia service for pets, and was this before or after the book developed?

A: It was in my first year of practicing veterinary medicine, about the same time as I started writing my book, when I came to the realization that my profession was not adequately meeting the needs of owners when it came to providing a comfortable and anxiety free euthanasia for their pets.

My hospital received a letter from the owner of a mobile veterinary practice who stated that she could no longer provide home euthanasia services to animals unless they were pets of her existing clients. Her explanation was that the number of requests for at-home euthanasia was so overwhelming that she and her staff could no longer physically or emotionally meet the demand for them.

The problem became increasingly apparent to me over the course of my career. As a family veterinarian, I would receive calls from panicked clients who needed me to come out to their homes on an emergency basis to perform a euthanasia because they were unable to lift their large, now recumbent dog into the car. Many of my clients wanted me to come to their home because their elderly pet was terrified of the veterinarian. Rightfully so, they did not want its last hours to be spent frightened in an exam room at a veterinary hospital. Although all of us in the profession understand how important at-home euthanasia is to the owner and to the pet, the sad reality is that it is often impossible for veterinarians to leave their hospital to accommodate these requests. We are physically tied to our hospitals with a full day of scheduled appointments and surgeries on the books.

In recent years, I decided to start a veterinary organization which was exclusively devoted to providing an at-home euthanasia and cremation services to accommodate the need for the pets in our community. I knew that with the rising rate of burn-out, compassion fatigue, and suicides amongst veterinary professionals that if I started this service it needed to be fair to my colleagues as well. I could not put any one veterinary professional into a role whose sole job would be to euthanize animals all

week long. My solution was to create Gentle Goodbyes, an organization which is comprised of multiple veterinarians and technicians from different hospitals in the area who make themselves available through an on-call list. Thus, working together as a community of veterinary professionals, we can accommodate the need for home euthanasia seven days a week. The feedback from owners has been overwhelmingly positive and they are constantly letting us know how grateful they are to have this service available in their community. The veterinarians and technicians who are involved in our organization are also expressing how much easier and more compassionate they find euthanasia to be now that they are doing them within the home of the animal.

Q: How did you find the process of writing? Easy, Horrible? What made it work for you?

A: The process of writing the stories was the easy part. Most of my material came from simply observing the daily events that occurred while I was at work in the hospital. Veterinarians are frequently presented with emotionally charged and that frequency is magnified if you work in an emergency hospital. On any given day, I might find myself laughing, crying, feeling appalled, or feeling frightened for my safety and I drew upon those emotions to write my stories. It was the interactions that took place between the client and the vet, between the family members of the animals, or between the different veterinarians that were caring for the pet, that interested me the most and which ultimately became the focus of my stories. I wanted to present an unfiltered, uninhibited, behind the scenes look at the world of veterinary medicine so that pet owners and people who aspired to be veterinarians would have a true understanding of the demands and the stresses of the job. There seems to be a general misconception by the public that a veterinarian's days are spent vaccinating cute puppies and sewing up easily repaired

lacerations when in actuality, nothing could be further from the truth.

For me, the most difficult part of the process was organizing the stories into an order that would have continuity as a finished product. My stories were written over the span of many years. Each of my chapters describes an experience which is independent from the next chapter and which can stand alone as a story. In the end, I resolved the problem of how to organize the book by physically printing the stories out and then lining the piles of paper up along the floor of my living room. I then shuffled the chapters, and arranged and rearranged them, until I found an order that I thought would work best to tell the overall story.

It was not the most sophisticated solution but it worked. When I read the book in its final sequence I realized that the reason that it worked was because it's format mimicked the daily life of a veterinarian. Veterinarians schedules tend to change rapidly and our roles will morph quickly when moving from one patient to the next. We may have appointments that take longer than they should, surgeries that don't go as planned, or oversized, combative dogs that won't passively cooperate as we try to trim their nails. A single x-ray of a vomiting dog may send us scrambling to find a block of time in our schedule where we can get into the operating room to remove the tennis ball that is lodged halfway down his intestinal tract. During any single shift, we may find ourselves acting as cardiologists, radiologists, surgeons, ophthalmologists, dentists or grief counselors. Our days are in constant flux and we reorganize our days frequently to accommodate the needs of our patients. Ultimately, I found that the end order of the chapters in my book matched the pace, the tempo, and the random disarray which makes up a typical day in the life of a veterinarian.

Q: How has the response from readers

been?

A: The part that both surprised and delighted me was how varied the responses were to my book. It was remarkable to me that not one person recounted the same story twice, and that everyone I spoke to seemed to remember the book as having had a different emotional impact on them. One person remarked how she had "out-and-out belly laughs" while reading through it, another told me how she had cried over the story of the geriatric, aggressive chihuahua that I had taken into my home and tried to rehabilitate. Another expressed how angry she was about the verbal abuse that veterinarians are subject to, another mentioned how utterly disgusting she found the stories about abscesses to be. I can't disagree with her there, abscesses truly are nauseating. A few told me they could never look at a dog with a docked tail in the same way again. A close friend swore he would never breed a dog again after having read my book. My internal response to the latter set of feedback was …good! I may have actually managed to educate a few readers about some of the ethical dilemmas that we face as veterinarians. It delights me that the responses to my book would have created such a wide range of reactions in the people who have read it. Surely, that must be a sign that it is not a boring read.

In the reviews that were left Online, the response that was reiterated with the most frequency was that it was a "fun and heartbreaking" read. Hmmm, fun and heartbreaking. If that is the response that I elicited in the average reader then I feel vindicated that I did my job correctly because that is exactly how most veterinarians feel about their jobs. Overwhelmingly, the majority of reviews supported and cheered me on. "Screamingly funny", "teaches and enlightens", "sincere and uplifting", "a very realistic portrayal", "a must read for every pet owner", "engrossing" and "makes you laugh and makes want to tear your hair out" were just a few of the myriad of responses that I got.

Of course, there were the on-line readers who I clearly failed to impress. "BORING" and "now I'm depressed" and the very descriptive and emphatic single word "Yuck!". All of which, I have to admit, made me rethink my career as a writer. Luckily, these unflattering sentiments were a small minority of the reviews and which ultimately did not dissuade me from continuing my pursuit to become a better writer. And finally, a sincere and gracious thank you to the anonymous on-line woman who reads two hundred and fifty books a year and whose favorite animal book is "All Creatures Great and Small" by James Herriot. Her comment that "this book

is a close second [to my book Bite Me] made me laugh and cry with compassion and joy," truly made me sit down on the nearest chair that I could find and cry with my own tears of joy. I could not imagine a greater compliment than a comparison to this writer who, when I was just a small child, sparked my own budding interest in a profession which I eventually chose to be my own.

Q: Do you have plans for any additional books?

A: I have a never-ending pile of stories, which are in various phases of completion, stacked up on my desk. For as long as I continue to practice veterinary medicine I am sure that the stories will continue to flow. For my next book, one of my main goals is to sit down with my colleagues who practice less conventional dairy, equine, or zoo medicine and ask them questions that they would never dare to answer if it was not being asked by a fellow colleague. I want to show the reality version of those facets of veterinary medicine and to highlight some of the challenges that these doctors face. I also want to interview my colleagues who practice small animal medicine along with me and pass on their messages of what they would want the general public to know about our profession. The art of veterinary medicine is not just my story and I think that the world should hear their honest perspective as well.

Lastly, I want to continue to include the life lessons that I have learned while traveling throughout this planet. I have spent a good part of my life traveling to remote and untraveled destinations. People who know me well have endlessly encouraged me to write a book about my travel adventures. Others have encouraged me to write about my professional life. In Bite Me, I chose to combine stories from both aspects. I included the experiences that I had with the medical care that is available to humans in third world countries and I compared it to the high technology care that is available for animals in developed countries. Interweaving these travel tales into my book served the purpose of giving the reader a much-needed break from the sights, sounds and smells that occur when living within the walls of a veterinary hospital. In my next book, I would like to continue that theme because I have so many stories to tell about both.

Or on second thought, perhaps I'll write a romance novel… Just kidding.

KIRKUS BOOK REVIEW

BITE ME Tell-All Tales of an Emergency

Veterinarian Laura Lefkowitz Self (244 pp.) $9.50 paperback, $3.49 e-book ISBN: 978-0-692-60234-8; December 20, 2015

A collection of essays captures the unpredictable, demanding life of an emergency veterinarian.

Lefkowitz (Did My Dog Eat a Sock? Did My Dog Eat a Rock?, 2014), a veterinarian for more than 20 years, currently practices outside Boise, Idaho. From veterinary school onward, she's been jotting down peculiar professional moments. In such a stressful career—vets are disproportionately likely to commit suicide, she notes—it's important to look for the lighter side. Whether it's a kitten swallowing a condom or a dog sipping piña coladas, she often shakes her head over owner negligence and animal mischief.

"My job is never boring," the author proclaims. The book's careful thematic structure also reflects the fact that diagnoses tend to bunch together. On "The Night of Traumas," for instance, she treated a farm cat with an amputated lower leg, a dachshund hit by a car, and a feline attacked by two dogs. An edgy chapter on sex cannily pulls together disparate anecdotes: canine penis problems, the collection of semen from farm animals, customers' touchiness about pets' gender, and a sexual harassment charge she filed against a male technician. Indeed, many stories involve people's odd behavior rather than animals'; the author renders in italics the often sarcastic responses she keeps to herself. Although it was heartbreaking to give owners bad news, Lefkowitz maintained a detached perspective when euthanizing several animals a day. On the other hand, she gave her heart to the elderly Chihuahua and accident-prone poodle she adopted.

Neatly weaving in autobiographical snippets, Lefkowitz remembers her father's sudden death and her mother's severe injuries when hit by a car. Family tragedies prepared her for emergency situations and taught her to seize the day: she and her partner traveled the world by bike, marveling at how African doctors coped with equipment inferior to that in American veterinary clinics. The 13 black-and-white photographs are a nice addition, but minor typos (for example, "supercede" for "supersede") and punctuation issues ("cars ignition," instead of "car's ignition") detract slightly from the overall quality. Apart from a somewhat cheesy final chapter punning on tails/tales, these fun, good-natured vignettes are well chosen.

Witty stories about caring for animals that delicately balance comedy and pathos.

BOOKSHOP 'N PIECES

Authors: Feature your published book here. Please email us: info@booksnpieces.com and include a **high-resolution (300 dpi)** cover image, a brief synopsis and the links to your book.

Losing Cadence by Laura Lovett

When Cadence Weaverly graduates from high school, she thinks it's for the best that she and her boyfriend, Richard White, take separate paths: she to Julliard and he back to Harvard. Ten years later, she has an ideal job and a wonderful fiancé, Christian.

She is building the life of her dreams-until the day Richard resurfaces out of the blue, abducts her from her San Francisco apartment, and returns her to his mansion where he holds her captive. In this psychological thriller, a young woman must rely on perseverance, courage, and inner strength to survive after she is kidnapped by her deranged ex-boyfriend.

Buy it at Amazon.com: https://amzn.to/2JZIiI5

The Progeny by Tosca Lee

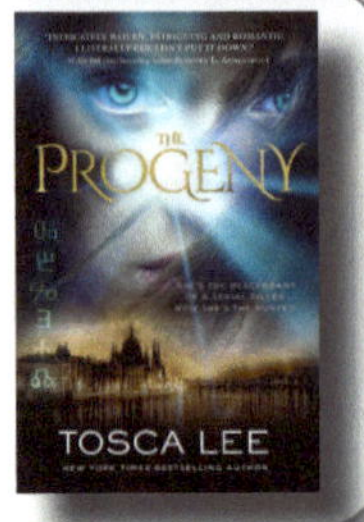

Elizabeth Bathory, the most notorious female serial killer of all time. Emily Jacobs is the descendant of a serial killer. Now, she's become the hunted. She's on a quest that will take her to the secret underground of Europe and the inner circles of three ancient orders—one determined to kill her, one devoted to keeping her alive, and one she must ultimately save. Filled with adrenaline, romance, and reversals, The Progeny is the present-day saga of a 400-year-old war between the uncanny descendants of "Blood Countess"

Elizabeth Bathory, the most prolific female serial killer of all time, and a secret society dedicated to erasing every one of her descendants. It is a story about the search for self filled with centuries-old intrigues against the back drop of atrocity and hope. Buy it at Amazon.com: https://amzn.to/2AibnPm

First Born by Tosca Lee

From New York Times bestselling author Tosca Lee comes the much-anticipated, high-speed sequel to The Progeny, about the powerful descendants of Elizabeth Bathory, the most prolific serial killer of all time. Face-to-face with her past, Audra Ellison now knows the secret she gave up everything—including her memory—to protect. A secret made vulnerable by her rediscovery, and so powerful neither the Historian nor the traitor Prince Nikola will ever let her live to keep it. Audra only has one impossible chance: find and kill the Historian and end the centuries old war between the Progeny and Scions at last—all while running from the law powers in a final bid to save them all and put her powers to the ultimate test. Love, action, and stunning revelation reign in this thrilling conclusion to The Progeny. Buy it on Amazon.com: https://amzn.to/2LviV6g

The Fire of Orc by Tony Phillips

In the wasted world, what does an old man remember? Before the fires he was part of something, something that would last. So he thought. Looking back fifty years to the destruction of 2032, he knows the end was inevitable. Power, greed, ambition and murder were the order of the day – and then the fires. A survivor remembers how the dawn of quantum computing signaled the end of democracy, how lust, vengeance and scandal lit the fuse, and how a hardened few started over, rebuilding tomorrow from the ruins of yesterday.

Fans of George Orwell, Philip K. Dick and Ursula Le Guin will recognize and appreciate the scope of this post-apocalyptic thriller.

Buy it on Amazon.com: https://amzn.to/2K0uywL

Shattered by McKensie Stewart

Emily finds herself metaphorically waking up to face a life she no longer recognizes. She loves her husband Brendon Graham, the Senator for the State of Pennsylvania along with their twins Madison and Connor but that isn't enough any longer. Even though Emily only shared part of her secret with Brendon; he is on a destructive spiral choosing escorts, booze and heroine to cope with the pain he feels from their loss. Kyndall, the matriarch of the family, and Emily's mother-in-law will do everything in her power to ensure that her dream of Brendon becoming the President of the United States will come to fruition no matter who she has to kill to make it happen. Emily's true love, Julia, her college roommate has a huge secret of her own that will shatter any reconciliation between the two of them. Buy it at Amazon.com: https://amzn.to/2mQ9OP0

All That Remains by Robin Melhuish

A tale of circumstance, a chance find in a junk shop and an old war vet's tale that leads to the love of Alastair's life and uncovers a trail of lies and deceit that goes back decades. The devious connivance of the unscrupulous, on all sides, in WWII to defraud their nations of millions before the war ends. The story of babies bred for the Third Reich and the mothers that gave their bodies, some more freely than others. Then love gets in the way, the rest is history. A family branded by the sins of the past a woman tormented by love and deception. All leading to the discovery of the worlds greatest undiscovered robbery.

It's all smoke and mirrors, it's all fake, or is it? Why did they wait 30 years before telling the story?

Buy it on Amazon.com: https://amzn.to/2LTp3l4

BOOKSHOP 'N PIECES

YEGman by Konn Lavery

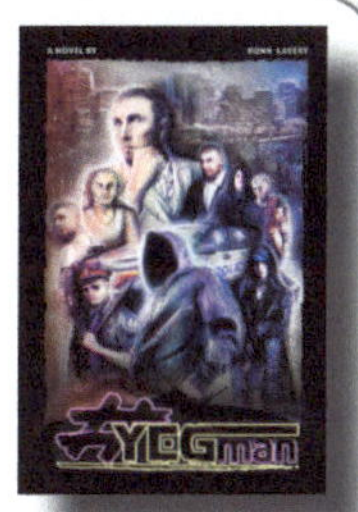

In the darkest streets of Edmonton, crime is around every corner. The police have exhausted their resources. Citizens are in a constant state of fear. The city is in dire need of justice. Someone needs to give the felons what they deserve – skip the courts and deliver their verdict with a fist full of fury! At least that is what Michael Bradford tells himself. He struggles with violent tendencies while personally investigating the Crystal Moths, Edmonton's most notorious gang. His vigilante methods get caught on film and are uploaded to the web with the hashtag YEGman. These videos catch the attention of a rebellious journalism student whose aspires to cover the developing story on the city's underground hero. Buy it at Amazon.com: https://amzn.to/2Iowpvn

Quantum Night by Robert J. Sawyer - 2017 AURORA AWARD FOR BEST NOVEL

Now, this Hugo and Nebula Award-winning author explores the thin line between good and evil that every human being is capable of crossing...Experimental psychologist Jim Marchuk has developed a flawless technique for identifying the previously undetected psychopaths lurking everywhere in society. But while being cross-examined about his breakthrough in court, Jim is shocked to discover that he has lost his memories of six months of his life from twenty years previously–a dark time during which he himself committed heinous acts.

As a rising tide of violence and hate sweeps across the globe, the psychologist and the physicist combine forces in a race against time to see if they can do the impossible–change human nature–before the entire world descends into darkness. Buy it at Amazon.com: https://amzn.to/2GgmKoB

The Forgotten Ones by Steena Holmes

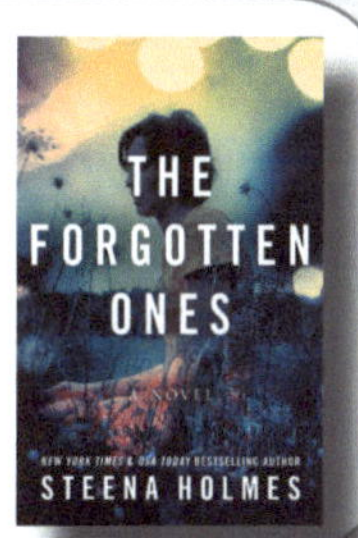

A spellbinding novel about an unspeakable secret that could destroy a family, from the New York Times bestselling author of Finding Emma. Elle is a survivor. She's managed to piece together a solid life from a childhood of broken memories and fairy tales her mom told her to explain away bad dreams. But weekly visits to her mother still fill Elle with a paralyzing fear she can't explain. It's just another of so many unanswered questions she grew up with in a family estranged by silence and secrets.Elle's world turns upside down when she receives a deathbed request from her grandfather, a man she was told had died years ago. As Elle's past unfolds, so does the truth—if she can believe it. She must face the reasons for her inexplicable dread. As dark as they are, Elle must listen…before her grandfather's death buries the family's secrets forever. Buy it on Amazon.com: https://amzn.to/2IlNTIC

Freedom Broker by K.J. Howe

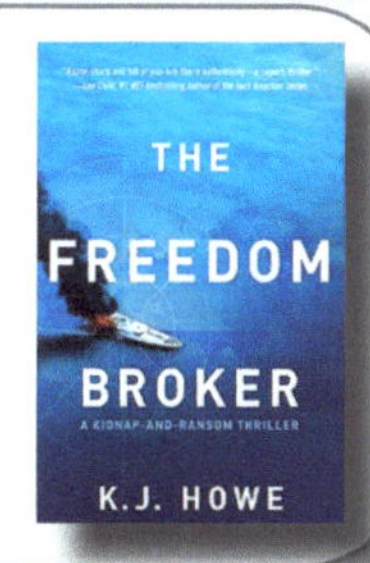

There are twenty-five elite kidnap and ransom (K&R) specialists in the world. Only one is a woman: Thea Paris. Twenty years ago, a terrified young boy was abducted in the middle of the night by masked intruders while his sister watched, paralyzed with fear. Returned after a harrowing nine months with his captors, Thea's brother has never been the same. Her childhood nightmare resurfaces when her oil magnate father, Christos Paris, is snatched from his yacht off Santorini on his sixtieth birthday. The brutal kidnappers left the entire crew slaughtered in their wake, but strangely, there are no ransom demands, no political appeals, no prisoner release requests-just obscure and foreboding texts written in Latin sent from burner phones. Will she be able to prevent this kidnapping from destroying her family for good? Buy it at Amazon.com: https://amzn.to/2IkccGM

A Beautiful Glittering Lie by J.D.R. Hawkins

In the spring of 1861, a country once united is fractured by war. Half of America chooses to fight for the Confederate cause; the other, for unification. In north Alabama, the majority favors remaining in the Union, but when the state secedes, many come to her defense.

Such is the case with Hiram Summers, a farmer and father of three. He decides to enlist, and his son, David, also desires to go, but is instead obligated to stay behind. Buy it at Amazon.com: https://amzn.to/2mP6tj6

Ares by K.A. Finn

Gryffin was the sole survivor of The Foundation's experimental project to transform human children into hybrid cyborgs - half human, half machine. The program failed and he was sent on a one way trip into The Outer Sector where he was left for dead. He has survived for twenty years by suppressing his human emotions and embracing his machine side. When Gryffin saves Officer Terra Rush from an attack, Terra uncovers a terrible secret. The Foundation has been lying to her...and maybe they still are. They have labelled Gryffin a killing machine, yet he acts more human than many of The Foundation's leaders. Can Gryffin overcome the machine inside and trust her? Or will getting in touch with his human emotions destroy him once and for all?

Buy it on Amazon.com: https://amzn.to/2uVp7dG

BOOKSHOP 'N PIECES

Wham (Timewalker Book 1) by Carol Marrs Phipps

When Children and Family Assistance police drag her mom, her dad and her beautiful sister out the door into the night and beat her senseless, Tess Greenwood finds herself alone, her every move watched by the hidden World Alliance. Almost blind after her beating, she flees to the forbidden Broadstreet compound and a troll named Maxi.

So begins Tess's journey from quiet teen at home to fierce young woman, determined to get back her family any way she can. Even if she must travel time itself. But time is one thing she has little of. Those arrested in the night seldom live for long, and beautiful young women are destined to become toys for the elite.

Frantic, Tess tries to pull herself together to save her loved ones and her world... and the clock is ticking.

Buy it at Amazon.com: https://amzn.to/2Oq9W4m

The Children's Game: A Thriller by Max Karpov

The CIA has learned that the Kremlin is about to launch a sophisticated propaganda operation aimed at discrediting and disrupting the United States and ultimately restoring Russia to great nation status. Intercepted intelligence suggests that the operation will hinge on a single, breaking news event in Eastern Europe, supported by a sustained campaign of disinformation and cyberattacks. Code-named the "Children's Game"--a chess stratagem that leads to checkmate in four moves--it was probably conceived by a Russian billionaire and former FSB officer named Andrei Turov. But the United States has its own secret weapon: Christopher Niles, a former CIA intelligence officer, who understands Turov's ambitions and capabilities. He must restore truth to a world spiraling into chaos. Buy it at Amazon.com: https://amzn.to/2uXx0zj

Ruler of the Night (Thomas and Emily De Quincey) by David Morrell

1855. The railway has irrevocably altered English society, effectively changing geography and fueling the industrial revolution by shortening distances between cities: a whole day's journey can now be covered in a matter of hours. People marvel at their new freedom. But train travel brings new dangers as well, with England's first death by train recorded on the very first day of railway operations in 1830. Twenty-five years later, England's first train murder occurs, paralyzing London with the unthinkable when a gentleman is stabbed to death in a safely locked first-class passenger compartment. In the next compartment, the brilliant opium-eater Thomas De Quincey must confront two ruthless adversaries: this terrifying enemy, and his own opium addiction which endangers his life and his tormented soul. Buy it on Amazon.com: https://amzn.to/2LWwVSQ

The Seventh Plague: A Sigma Force Novel by James Rollins

If the biblical plagues of Egypt truly happened--could they happen again--on a global scale? Two years after vanishing into the Sudanese desert, the leader of a British archeological expedition, Professor Harold McCabe, comes stumbling out of the sands, frantic and delirious, but he dies before he can tell his story. The mystery deepens when an autopsy uncovers someone had begun to mummify the professor's body while he was still alive. Professor McCabe had vanished into the desert while searching for proof of the ten plagues of Moses. Sigma Force will confront a threat born of the ancient past and made real by the latest science--a danger that will unleash a cascading series of plagues, culminating in a scourge that could kill all of the world's children . . . decimating mankind forever. Are those plagues starting again? Buy it on Amazon.com: https://amzn.to/2uXBPsx

Bishop's War (Bishop Series Book 1) by Rafael Amadeus Hines

This fast-paced and action-packed suspense thriller introduces us to Special Forces Sergeant John Bishop, decorated war hero, and nephew of crime boss, Gonzalo Valdez. After returning home from Afghanistan John's hopes for a peaceful future are quickly shattered when he is catapulted back into the global war on terror through a succession of life-threatening events and corrupt intrigue. He battles against terrorist operatives in New York, a powerful Afghan warlord, and a psychopathic billionaire with powerful White House connections.

This is a thriller not to be matched for intensity and breathless excitement—not for the faint-hearted.

Buy it at Amazon.com: https://amzn.to/2NSO4gK

The Lost Order: (Cotton Malone) by Steve Berry

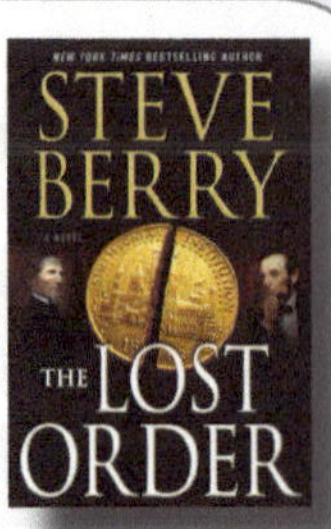

The Knights of the Golden Circle was the largest and most dangerous clandestine organization in American history. It amassed billions in stolen gold and silver, all buried in hidden caches across the United States. Since 1865 treasure hunters have searched, but little of that immense wealth has ever been found.

Now, one hundred and sixty years later, two factions of what remains of the Knights of the Golden Circle want that lost treasure—one to spend it for their own ends, the other to preserve it. From the backrooms of the Smithsonian to the deepest woods in rural Arkansas, and finally up into the rugged mountains of northern New Mexico, The Lost Order by Steve Berry is a perilous adventure into our country's dark past, and a potentially even darker future. Buy it on Amazon.com: https://amzn.to/2OtgTBM

BOOKSHOP 'N PIECES

Skyjack: (A Thea Paris Novel) by K.J. Howe

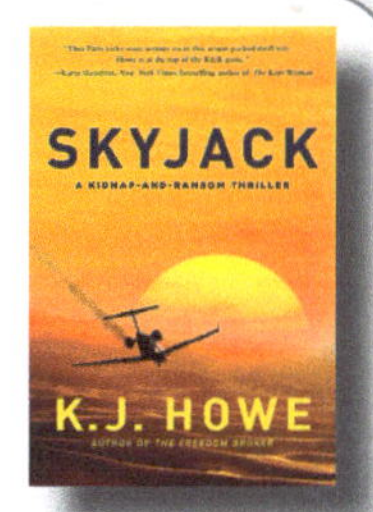

In the follow-up to her exhilarating debut, The Freedom Broker, K.J. Howe delivers a "riveting" and "rip-roaring" thriller perfect for fans of Sandra Brown and Lisa Gardner. International kidnap expert Thea Paris is escorting two former child soldiers on a plane from an orphanage in Kanzi, Africa, to adoptive parents in London when the Boeing Business Jet is hijacked and forced to make an emergency landing in the remote Libyan desert. Revealing a deadly conspiracy that connects the dark postwar legacy of World War II to the present, this case will bring all parties to an explosive conclusion that will decide the fate of millions across Europe and the Middle East.

  Buy it at Amazon.com: https://amzn.to/2Ls8O2a

Testimony by Scott Turow

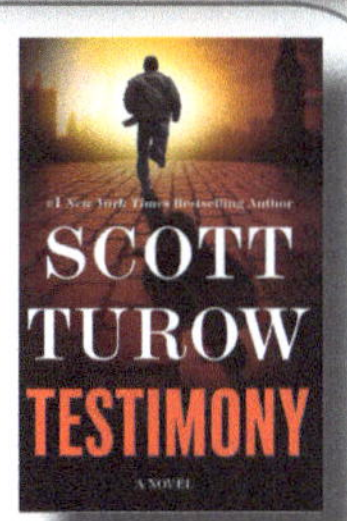

At the age of fifty, former prosecutor Bill ten Boom has walked out on everything he thought was important to him: his law career, his wife, Kindle County, even his country. Still, when he is tapped by the International Criminal Court--an organization charged with prosecuting crimes against humanity--he feels drawn to what will become the most elusive case of his career. Over ten years ago, in the apocalyptic chaos following the Bosnian war, an entire Roma refugee camp vanished. Only Ferko survived. Boom's task is to examine Ferko's claims and determinine who might have massacred the Roma. A master of the legal thriller, Scott Turow has returned with his most irresistibly confounding and satisfying novel yet.

  Buy it at Amazon.com: https://amzn.to/2Lvo3rk

Mississippi Blood: (The Natchez Burning Trilogy) by Greg Iles

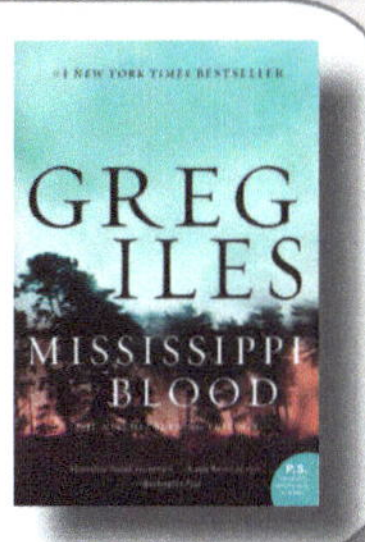

  The endgame is at hand for Penn Cage, his family, and the enemies bent on destroying them in this revelatory volume in the epic trilogy set in modern-day Natchez, Mississippi—Greg Iles's epic tale of love and honor, hatred and revenge that explores how the sins of the past continue to haunt the present. Shattered by grief and dreaming of vengeance, Penn Cage sees his family and his world collapsing around him. Unable to trust anyone around him--not even his own mother--Penn joins forces with Serenity Butler, a famous young black author who has come to Natchez to write about his father's case. Together, Penn and Serenity battle to crack the Double Eagles and discover the secret history of the Cage family and the South itself, a desperate move that risks the only thing they have left to gamble: their lives. Buy it on Amazon.com: https://amzn.to/2LEfSIz

End Game (Will Robie Series) by David Baldacci

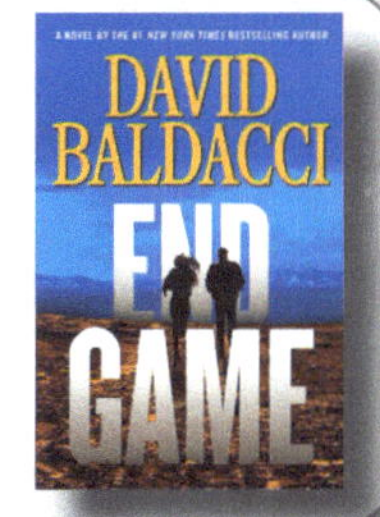

  Will Robie and Jessica Reel are two of the most lethal people alive. They're the ones the government calls in when the utmost secrecy is required to take out those who plot violence and mass destruction against the United States. And through every mission, one man has always had their backs: their handler, code-named Blue Man.

  But now, Blue Man is missing. Sent to investigate, Robie and Reel arrive in the small town of Grand to discover that it has its own share of problems. But lying in wait in Grand is an even more insidious and sweeping threat, one that may shake the very foundations of America. And when Robie and Reel find themselves up against an adversary with superior firepower and a home-court advantage, they'll be lucky if they make it out alive, with or without Blue Man. Buy it on Amazon.com: https://amzn.to/2uZCPMw

Amazonia by James Rollins

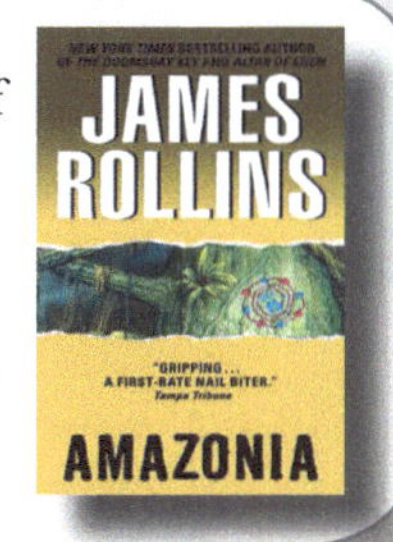

  The Rand scientific expedition entered the lush wilderness of the Amazon and never returned. Years later, one of its members has stumbled out of the world's most inhospitable rainforest—a former Special Forces soldier, scarred, mutilated, terrified, and mere hours from death, who went in with one arm missing . . . and came out with both intact. Unable to comprehend this inexplicable event, the government sends Nathan Rand into this impenetrable secret world. But the nightmare that is awaiting Nate and his team of scientists and seasoned U.S. Rangers dwarfs any danger they anticipated . . . an ancient, unspoken terror—a power beyond human imagining—that can forever alter the world beyond the dark, lethal confines of . . .

  Buy it at Amazon.com: https://amzn.to/2Ak7sS2

Beneath a Scarlet Sky by Mark Sullivan

  Pino Lella wants nothing to do with the war or the Nazis. He's a normal Italian teenager—obsessed with music, food, and girls—but his days of innocence are numbered. When his family home in Milan is destroyed by Allied bombs, Pino joins an underground railroad helping Jews escape over the Alps, and falls for Anna, a beautiful widow six years his senior. In an attempt to protect him, Pino's parents force him to enlist as a German soldier—a move they think will keep him out of combat. Now, with the opportunity to spy for the Allies inside the German High Command, Pino endures the horrors of the war and the Nazi occupation by fighting in secret, his courage bolstered by his love for Anna and for the life he dreams they will one day share.

  Buy it on Amazon.com: https://amzn.to/2uWrVXY